THE BRANCHES
we
CHERISH

An Open Adoption Memoir

Note: This is a true and accurate story. While many names have been changed to protect the families' privacy, we want to share our gift of open adoption and demonstrate the importance of relationships between birth and adoptive families.

Linda R. Sexton

Adoptive Parent and Open Adoption Pathfinder,
with reflections from adopted children, birth mothers,
birth fathers, and birth grandmothers

THE BRANCHES
we
CHERISH

An Open Adoption Memoir

GAUDIUM

Gaudium Publishing

Las Vegas ◊ Chicago ◊ Palm Beach

Published in the United States of America by
Histria Books
7181 N. Hualapai Way, Ste. 130-86
Las Vegas, NV 89166 U.S.A
HistriaBooks.com

Gaudium Publishing is an imprint of Histria Books. Titles published under the imprints of Histria Books are distributed worldwide.

Library of Congress Control Number: 2023948271

ISBN 978-1-59211-381-1 (hardcover)
ISBN 978-1-59211-402-3 (eBook)

Contents

Prologue 9

PART I — Meet the Branches 15

    1. So Many Questions 15

    2. North Star 19

PART II — Matching with Expecting Parents 24

    3. The Book 24

    4. The First Phone Call 30

    5. Leap of Faith 32

    6. Matched Again 42

    7. Raistlin 55

PART III — The Births 66

    8. A Heavy Weight 66

    9. First Forty-Eight Hours 75

PART IV— Parenting Journey Begins 80

    10. Change of Plan 80

    11. Monthly Reports 84

    12. Not a Special Aunt 99

    13. Making Time 101

    14. He Matters. *Includes special feature by Ricky, birth father* 112

PART V- Growing Up 122

    15. Babies Grieve 122

    16. Machu Picchu 131

    17. Big Sister Sofie 134

    18. Profound Connection. *Includes feature interview with my two*
        adopted children 138

PART VI — Birth Family Reflections 149

    19. A Satori Experience. *Includes special feature by Jenna, birth mother* 149

    20. Changed Lives 162

    21. Eighteen Gifts. *Includes special feature by Beth, birth grandmother* 168

PART VII — Closing Thoughts 172

    22. Not Yet Earned 172

    23. Adult Choice 175

    24. No Longer Afraid 177

Afterword 180

Appendix 183

Acknowledgments 187

Dedicated with love, respect, and deepest gratitude
to birth parents Jenna, Michael, Rachel, and Ricky.

To my children Finley and Sofie. You are my everything.

To David, my brave partner, husband,
and our family touchstone.

Prologue

"We do not know."

— Adoption Counselor, 1993

Open Adoption: an adoption arrangement in which the biological parents and the adoptive family know each other's identities and choose to remain in contact after the adoption process is finalized.

The first time I held my adopted child, I was absolutely overcome with love — just like any other parent. That was the easy part, never even a question. But in the days, weeks, months, and years to come, questions did arise, many of which I had no easy answer to. Most times we just followed our internal compass, our gut-feeling if you will, that told us that keeping our child connected to their birth family was a good healthy choice. That choice has served us very well.

I came by the title of this book one beautiful sunny Sunday morning, sitting in our church's cemetery field. For months, our weekly service was conducted outdoors due to the pandemic. I grew to love the solitude of gathering together yet sitting utterly alone in my thoughts with no expectations of connecting with anyone.

That morning, I looked up and there was this giant, imperfect tree with a strong trunk and two great distinct branches on either side. I thought, *This is us!* One big, beautiful, whole tree. In the center are our two children, Finley and Sofie, my husband, David, me, grandparents, aunts, uncles, and cousins. The great forked branch to the left represents Finley's birth parents, Jenna and Michael, and their children and families. And the great forked branch to the right represents Sofie's birth parents, Rachel and Ricky, and their children and families. We are all connected in this family tree. And we cherish every single branch.

The fact that over seventy percent of adoptions today are open to some extent versus closed is not well known. How open adoption works is even less understood. Closed adoptions and sealed records are still common knowledge in our society and because many people automatically assume adoption is closed and secretive, they have a dim view of adoption. We have all heard stories about adoptees searching for where they came from and longing to know their birth families. We have heard the stories of birth mothers and birth fathers longing to know about the child they placed for adoption years ago. It does not have to be that way.

When we decided to pursue an open adoption, we had so many questions. How did it work? How did you match with an expecting mother? What were the chances of finding an expecting mother considering adoption? How many couples were looking to adopt versus expecting mothers making an adoption plan? What happened before the baby was born? At the hospital? After placement? While the agency could answer many questions about the process early on, they could tell us little about the long-term relationships between adoptive and birth families.

As of this writing, Finley is twenty-eight, and Sofie is twenty-four years old. I remember asking my adoption counselor, "What happens in the first year? First five years? Twenty years later?" Since open adoption was still so new, her answer was a simple, "We do not know."

My biggest fear was that the birth parents would want to be too involved. What were we getting ourselves into? At that time, the agency had only been doing open adoptions for about three years, so there wasn't a lot they could tell us. The counselor simply said, "We will help you make a plan for the first six months. It will not be a legally binding contract, but it will be an agreement for contact and/or visitation. After that, it is all up to you."

What a scary thought.

Over time, though, we discovered that we wanted our children's birth parents in our lives — for them and for us. And the roles of parents and birth parents became clear, and boundaries were never crossed. We were able to forge comfortable — although not always perfect — relationships and our love for each other grew over the years. Both Finley and Sofie want to share their birth family journeys to help inform others who come after them.

In the beginning, we also did not understand some of the complexities of raising adopted children and naively thought that if we adopted an infant, raising that child would be no different from giving birth to them. We did not fully appreciate the trauma of adoption to the child or to the birth families.

What I have come to understand is that everyone in the adoption triad is vulnerable and often fragile when they come to the place of adoption.

For most adoptees, they had no voice in the adoption decision. No matter how wonderful, loving and understanding their adoptive family, they have lost the ability to grow up with the mom and dad and family who share their biological traits.

For the adoptive parent or parents, they are often dealing with their own infertility and perhaps even years of unsuccessful procreation and maybe even heartbreaking losses.

For the expecting parents, they have come to the adoption choice for a myriad of personal reasons — sometimes not even entirely of their own choosing. But whatever has brought them here, it is at a great cost of losing the ability to parent their child.

Beyond the adoption triad there are family members and close friends who share in these losses and vulnerabilities too. These are often the parents or siblings of the birth and adoptive families, and their role can be vital to the relationship dynamic. We refer to the whole of the people involved around the adopted person as the adoption constellation.

We had much to learn and understand about each other. There is a need to acknowledge the losses and vulnerabilities present in order to create space for the relationships to grow in a healthy manner. For us, much of it was intuitive as it relates to the importance of birth families, yet much was learned along the way, especially for our adopted children. For me, it has been a lifelong learning journey that has opened doors to enduring relationships and immeasurable love.

Any adoption, including open adoption, takes a lot of determination and guts. It takes a great deal of personal courage from both birth and adoptive families. It also takes time and patience. We were fortunate both times that it took a mere two to three years for each of our adoptions because it can often take longer. We applied to Methodist Mission Home in May 1993, and our first child, Finley, was born in November 1994. The Decree of Adoption was finalized in May 1995, almost two years exactly from the day we applied. We again applied to Methodist Mission Home in October 1996, and our daughter Sofie was born in September 1998. Her Decree of Adoption was finalized in March 1999, two years and five months from the day we applied. (Since then, Methodist Mission Home has changed its name to Providence Place, so that is how I will refer to them throughout this book.)

While our story follows the best practices at that time, much has evolved in the open adoption world. In fact, just by nature of being open and transparent, rather than closed, ours was considered the best and most ethical practice in the early 1990s. Yet some of what you will hear in our story, especially during the waiting and matching period, would not be considered best practice today. The adoption industry is evolving to be more centric to the needs and rights of expecting parents (especially minors) and adopted children and continues to struggle to get it right. There are efforts to shift the focus to making adoption more about finding families for babies and children that need homes, rather than what some would describe as a practice of finding babies or children for waiting adoptive parents.

For years the narrative of adoption has been written by the adoptive families and adoption agencies. Now, the voices of adoptees and birth parents are beginning to emerge. While this memoir is written from my perspective as an adoptive parent many years ago, I have taken care to incorporate the voices of everyone involved in our story. Included are features written by a birth father, a birth mother, and a birth grandmother. Some of this material comes from the extensive notes I took during our first adoption, but much of it comes from our memories, adoption documents, and interviews with my adult children and their birth parents. My children's birth parents were all teenagers during their unplanned pregnancies, so their perspective is especially relevant for young expecting parents, and not unique to teens only. This memoir will also be helpful to the counselors and therapists who guide birth parents, adoptive parents, and adoptees through these challenging yet rewarding relationships. You will learn about the fears, pain, and indescribable joys of our open adoption. There is not a day that goes by that we are not grateful for this journey. In the following pages, you will find that our birth-family relationships are built on mutual trust, respect, deep gratitude for one another, and, most importantly, love for the children.

PART I – Meet the Branches

1. So Many Questions

"There is no greater trust than an expecting parent choosing you to raise their child."

— David, adoptive father

Little did I know that I would become an open adoption pathfinder. When we married, David and I knew that we might not be able to have children. Yet, during our marriage preparation meeting, when the pastor asked us if we wanted to keep the part about the procreation of children in our vows, we said without hesitation, "Yes!" But procreation was not meant to be for us.

I was thirty-two by the time I met the man I had been looking for. He was intelligent, stable, funny, and kind, and by our second date, I knew I wanted to marry him. But as life happens, my work transferred me from Houston to Dallas just as our relationship was going strong.

In those days, an up-and-coming airline — Southwest — was making a name for itself in the Texas market. They sold coupon books with nineteen-dollar one-way tickets between Houston and Dallas, with flights scheduled every thirty minutes. When the work week was done, one of us would head to the airport and hop on the next flight. How easy was that. It was even more economical to fly than to drive. Those were fun, magical days full of airport kisses. To this day, our airport greeting kisses remain our special treat. We were both engineers for the same company, and once our wedding plans were set, the company transferred me back to Houston.

Married life was everything I had hoped and dreamed for. We had a great group of friends, loved each other's siblings, got along with our mothers-in-law, commuted to work together, and we were both enjoying our careers. In short order, we were ready to start our family. After some tries and failures, we naturally looked to adoption. It was an easy decision because we figured there were plenty of unplanned pregnancies, and if those babies needed a home, it could be a good solution for all. It seemed straightforward enough. What we have since learned is that adoption is far from simple for anyone who is part of the adoption constellation.

We soon learned that while the decision to adopt was easy, the actual process was not. At the time we were looking to adopt a baby there were many intercountry options available. However, we decided to try the private domestic adoption route rather than international, as we thought the domestic process might be easier and potentially faster.

To our dismay, many adoption agencies disqualified us, even though we were two professionals with stable jobs, good members of the community, and longtime churchgoers. So, what was the problem?

Our age.

By this time, I was thirty-six, and David was forty-three. The traditional adoption agencies said we were unfit to adopt because we were too old. But after interviewing seven adoption agencies, we learned that if we were willing to do an open adoption instead of a closed or semi-open one, we might qualify. We knew nothing about this term "open" adoption. A leading agency doing open adoptions at that time was Providence Place (formerly Methodist Mission Home) in San Antonio, Texas, a three-hour drive from our Houston residence. Off we went for the first of many visits to the agency.

We attended an introductory session with maybe five or six other hopeful couples and came away with information that changed our expectations and our lives. We began to understand what open adoption was about, and it felt beautiful. The expecting parents actually choose who raises their child. I later learned that we, too, would have choices to make.

We toured the Providence Place facility, which included rooms for expecting mothers to live in and even accommodations for other children if they had any. These women could live there regardless of whether they would make an adoption plan. But even back in 1993, few women resided there since the stigma of unwed mothers was disappearing. Many young women continued going to school, working at their jobs, and living in their homes during their pregnancies.

During that first information session, I was happy we weren't alone in that situation, but also a little concerned about the competition sitting next to us. At that time, there were about fifty waiting couples with this agency.

We wondered, *Who makes an adoption plan, and will we be able to relate to them?* That day, a guest speaker answered my question and left a lasting impression on me. She was the mother of a fifteen-year-old daughter who had placed her baby with a family in an open adoption arrangement. This birth grandmother appeared to be a kind, stable, and intelligent person. She explained that her teen, sitting next to her, could not raise a child, and the woman, too, was a single mother with other children. Neither one was in a position to take on the responsibility.

The birth mother was young and shy and didn't speak much, but I thought, *Wouldn't it be nice to match with someone like her?* I could tell how emotional and heartbreaking this was for mother and daughter. But they also seemed relieved that they had found a loving family and would stay connected. That's when we learned that open adoption is not only about choosing who parents your child; it's also about mutually deciding how to stay connected.

We still had so many questions: What does visitation between birth and adoptive families look like? Will it be awkward to raise a child with the birth parents in the picture? How do adopted children feel about this open arrangement? In the early 90's there was little guidance for these long-term relationships, and we needed to learn as we went.

Understanding the adoption triad is fundamental to our story. I found this explanation given by the Gladney Center for Adoption to be most helpful:

The adoption triad is composed of the three groups of people whose lives are joined as immediate members of an adoption family story. The first group in the triad is the birth parents. Even if one or both parents are unknown, they are still vital members of the triad. Children who were placed will always be a part of and forever linked to their birth parents.

The second part of the triad is the adoptive parent or parents. These parents will be the main caretakers of the child who has been placed and will have a very important role to fill. They are linked forever to their child through adoption, just as if they had conceived that child. They are also forever linked to the birth parents. Even if the adoption is closed, they will recognize glimmers of the birth parents in their child. They will also forever have the knowledge of the family that was created when the birth parents decided to place their child. If an adoption is open, this relationship and bond can hopefully continue to grow and flourish.

The last and most important part of the triad is the child placed for adoption. This child will be bonded and joined forever with both birth and adoptive parents. Adopted children will have traits of both families and will always have a connection to each in a deeper way than any other member of the triad could understand. They will learn how to navigate through life from their adoptive parents and about their heritage through the conversations or stories of their birth parents. If an adoption is closed, the child will still hold this connection through physical and natural traits.

The adoption triad is the triangle that binds an adoption story together for life.

2. North Star

"Open adoption changes adoption to being more about love than feeling like someone gave you away or abandoned you."

— Finley, adopted child

Central to the open-adoption experience is love and care for the child by all parties involved. Putting the child's well-being at the center of all relationships as the North Star helps guide everyone. So, it seems fitting to start by describing our children as young adults today.

Our first child, Finley, was born in Houston, Texas, to seventeen-year-old Jenna and seventeen-year-old Michael. Finley now lives in Austin, Texas, and is one of the bravest, most talented, complex, beautiful, and sensitive people I know. They gender identify as non-binary; an umbrella term for gender identity that is not solely male or female — identity that is outside the binary choice of male/female. Therefore, I will use the pronouns they/them/their throughout this book when referring to singular Finley. It takes practice to use they/them/their pronouns naturally and making sure my child is comfortable and supported is most important to me.

Throughout the school years, we lived in Vienna, Virginia, outside of Washington, D.C. Finley always had excellent grades, excelled in sports, had a strong interest in music and drawing, and had a great group of friends. But looking back, parenting was often a challenge. While I did not recognize adoption-related issues at the time, I can see them more clearly now. Something as simple as Finley not wanting to be hugged or comforted for too long is a classic sign that the adopted child is protecting their vulnerable self. And if there was ever a comment made about life after we — the parents — are gone, Finley had a visceral "never speak of that again" reaction — a sign of defending against further loss or abandonment.

These are some areas I will explore in future chapters. As you will see, we got through the challenging growing-up years, which were, in most aspects, not all that different from what many families go through, and in 2017, Finley graduated from Virginia Commonwealth University with a BA in Fine Arts.

After graduation, Finley decided to travel the world — often alone and sometimes with a partner. This was a difficult but necessary "letting go" time for us as parents. Finley was able to travel solo through workaway experiences. Overseas workaway means you agree to work in exchange for basic housing and some meals. Teaching English to Chinese students online was a great source of income while traveling too. Finley visited Peru, Costa Rica, Hawaii, the Philippines, Thailand, Vietnam, Australia, and Indonesia. And if it were not for the pandemic, Finley probably would still be traveling.

Finley's passions are promoting social and food justice, living a vegan lifestyle, growing plants, fostering kittens, and roller skating. Finley first became a vegetarian and, later, a vegan. Seeing a documentary in high school that depicted a meat production facility was all that was needed for Finley to stop consuming meat. Traveling in Asia was also a turning point to learn much more about veganism.

Finley returned to the United States and began making vegan cheeses. Giving up cheese was a big challenge moving from vegetarian to vegan, so Finley began to work on solutions. Peace Cheese, LLC, was founded and now entrepreneurial Finley sells vegan cheese to businesses and at farmers' markets and pop-up markets in Austin.

Finley is also working on getting closer to their birth parents. Austin is only a three-hour drive to the home of their birth parents, Jenna and Michael, who married each other in 2012 when Finley was seventeen. Remarkably, Jenna and Michael gave birth to a son in 2019, so Finley has a full-birth sibling who is twenty-five years younger.

Our second child, Sofie, was born in Austin, Texas, to fifteen-year-old Rachel and sixteen-year-old Ricky. She is a recent graduate of the University of Colorado Boulder and is the hardest working, most driven person I know, coupled with the sweetest disposition and kindest heart. Sofie lights up a room when she walks in and always has a kind word to share with everyone she meets. She has always been a perfectionist and has always excelled in school. She loves dogs, cats, the outdoors, thrifting, and is a natural leader.

Looking back with Sofie, too, I now see some traits that may have stemmed from adoption issues. Sofie was always the fixer in our family, the one to make everything right. She had a personality that everyone was attracted to. But occasionally, completely out of character, she would get so angry that she punched the wall! That baffled us as parents. We often asked ourselves, *Where did that anger come from?* I have now learned that many adoptees do harbor anger and are perhaps expressing a feeling that they have, do not understand, and are hiding out of fear of rejection.

In May 2021, Sofie earned her BS in Environmental Engineering and then an MS in Civil Engineering from CU Boulder. Her choice to attend college far from home was another difficult but necessary "letting go" experience for us.

Sofie is passionate about many things — first and foremost, the earth. She credits her love for taking care of the earth to Doctor Seuss's, *The Lorax*, which is about protecting the earth with the message: "Unless someone like you cares a whole awful lot, nothing is going to get better. It's not." The environment has been her passion since she was a little girl, and she is now making it her life mission. She is already honing her expertise in clean water and is working for an engineering consulting firm with the goal of making a difference in social and environmental justice.

In many ways, engineer Sofie could not be more different than her artist sibling; in other ways, they are inseparable. They are truly best friends. Both are human rights activists and animal lovers. Both are very creative, and they enjoy clothes, and hair and makeup fashion. Sofie has also caught the Colorado hiking, climbing, and camping bug and finds tremendous enjoyment in the outdoors. She has a strong desire for international travel like Finley and traveled to South America the summer after her graduation. Her workaway experience was at a dog shelter in Huanchaco, Peru. There, she grew her confidence in being independent and honed her Spanish language skills.

Sofie is also especially close to her birth father, Ricky, and his family. She always finds time to Facetime with her two younger birth siblings on his side. In addition, she has become a confidant and friend to two of her birth siblings on Rachel's side, who are now in middle and high school. They both, of course, look up to her. Sofie tries to take the time to call or text her birth siblings, no matter how busy life gets.

In preparing this story, I sat down to think about our visits with my children's birth families from the time we met and were matched until now. To my surprise and amazement, in thirty minutes, I jotted down twenty times I can recall visiting with Finley's birth family and twenty-eight times with Sofie's birth family. And I am sure I missed others. While I don't recall the specifics of all these visits, I do remember the feelings and emotions that accompanied them. We always antici-pated these interactions with excitement, but they were also an emotional drain on all of us. It is worth noting that we moved from Texas to Virginia when Finley was five and Sofie was one, so visits did require significant effort and travel.

Finley's birth family visits mostly occurred when they were a young child and usually with birth mother, Jenna, and sometimes another family member or friend. By the time we moved to Virginia, Jenna was thinking about starting a family. However, Jenna continued to visit us in Virginia until about the time Finley turned twelve. Finley's birth father, Michael, stayed in touch but only saw young three-year-old Finley once. Now as a young adult, Finley has visited both Jenna and Michael several times.

Sofie's birth family visits were more frequent and involved more participants since her birth father's family was very invested in our relationship. Visits often included birth grandparents, uncles, aunts, birth siblings, and even birth great-grandparents. Ricky's family was consistent with contact over the years. While we did not see Sofie's birth mother Rachel as often as we saw Ricky, she did visit, especially in the early years before she started to raise a family. And we traveled to Texas to visit with her, too, as Sofie was growing up. I always made an effort to ensure Sofie saw Rachel because I felt that the birth-mother connection was so important. I did not do the same for Finley with birth father Michael during the growing up years, and I consider that a miss and a regret.

What I can say about these visits with birth families are three very important things. First, the overarching emotions we experienced were love, gratitude, respect, and excitement to see each other. Second, Finley and Sofie were never confused about roles. They never questioned who their parents were. And finally, they loved seeing their birth families.

Our family tree is presented here to help you navigate our story.

PART II – Matching with Expecting Parents

3. The Book

"Birth parents aren't looking for the most attractive parents — they're looking for people they consider to be the best parents for their child..."

— The Open Adoption Experience, *Melina and Roszia*

When we entered the adoption world we discovered *The Book* — a large binder stuffed with Dear birth mother letters from hopeful adoptive couples and even some hopeful adoptive singles. It was overwhelming. We were required to create our own Dear birth mother letter, introducing ourselves to expecting mothers and telling them who we were, what our dreams and aspirations for a family were, and describing the kind of parents we wanted to be. (Today Dear Expecting Parent would be more appropriate than Dear birth mother because she is not a birth mother until she places her child.)

We also learned that we needed to send our Dear birth mother letter to at least one hundred friends and family, along with a cover letter explaining our desire to adopt and asking if they knew anyone with an unplanned pregnancy who was considering an adoption plan. *Wait a minute*, we thought. *Isn't it the agency's job to find these expecting mothers and help us match?* That's when we learned statistics about how many more hopeful adoptive couples than expecting mothers considering adoption there were. Whoa! How would this ever work?

The next thing we soon learned was that language was important. We were told to pay attention to language because these words have deep emotional meaning. We were counseled to avoid using the phrase *giving up*. When an expecting mother or father is considering adoption, they are *making an adoption plan* for their baby. They are not *giving their baby up* or *giving their baby away* for adoption. Those phrases have different meanings and elicit very different emotions. *Making an adoption plan* means being thoughtful, involved, and in control. And in open adoption, expecting parents think deeply about choosing the parents and family for their child.

The phrase, *giving your child up* or *giving your child away* implies much less connection and control. It feels as if you are handing your child over to someone else to decide their fate. We learned to always use the phrase, *making an adoption plan*. We really liked hearing this and it gave us a lot of confidence that the process and agency we chose would be ethical and transparent.

Some friends of ours — another waiting couple we had met during our visits to the agency — had been scammed by an attorney who claimed to be placing a baby for adoption. He showed them a sonogram, took their money, and after months of stringing them along, disappeared. Our radar was up that unethical adoptions were an issue.

Even though we were comfortable with the agency we chose, the idea of getting great photography for the book and networking was outside our comfort zone. However, we knew that expecting parents have many prospective adoptive parents to choose from, and the competition would be stiff, especially for placing infants. It made sense to us then that we needed to do this, so we dug deep, got comfortable with it, and went to work.

Simply browsing through *The Book* gave us pause. The couples all seemed so happy and confident — what competition we would face. And then it got worse. Not only did we need to write this compelling Dear birth mother letter, but we also needed to get great pictures — we wanted to look good — and young enough. We were already worried about age and being rejected again. In retrospect, our looks were the least of our worries, but it sure didn't feel like it at the time.

First, we had to apply and go through the formal vetting process. This included a home visit by the social worker; personal, employer, and even clergy references; physical exams; income tax and financial statements; marriage license; and a layout of our home. Then, we each completed an extensive written questionnaire package, which asked about our childhoods, marriage, employment, adoption expectations, infertility, extended families, religious development, child-rearing philosophy, and previous marriages and current children, if any. They also wanted to know how we negotiated conflict and managed finances.

We had to enlist friends and family members to vouch for us. But their statements were just the start because, in addition, we had to answer some tough questions. *Will you take only a newborn? Are you willing to adopt an older child? What about race? How important is that to you? And what if you are matched and the baby has significant health issues? Are you still willing to go through with the adoption? Are you willing to match with someone with no health insurance and pay all the costs? And sometimes expecting parents change their mind after the birth — are you prepared for that?* We were beginning to see the complexities of adoption.

Undeterred, we went about writing our Dear birth mother letter (letter in the appendix). It took weeks and many rewrites. We even tried to inject some humor, "We're both engineers but not nerds." We then solicited the help of David's brother, who was an advertising creative director at the time, to help make us look good. We knew that many expecting mothers considering adoption were young — even young teenagers. He searched the malls and went into the fashion shops for younger girls like the popular store at that time called Justice. He noted the in-vogue colors and dressed us in some clothes that made us look slightly more "hip" for the photos. I wore a jean jacket with lots of fun pins, and David wore a bright-yellow shirt. David's brother chose popular teen colors for our letter, and he added a sweet bear and some bees in lime green, teal, and yellow. We collected the names and addresses of friends, family, and colleagues, and soon our list was well over one hundred people. Once we got over the fact that we needed to announce our plans to the world, we were ready to send the letters. To our delight, our friends were very open and wanted to help.

With encouragement from the agency to network, and being the overachiever that I am, I even took some pretty green and yellow index cards, put sweet sparkly angel stickers on them with a message to contact me if you knew of any expecting mother considering adoption. Then I placed them on bulletin boards around our community. We even purchased a special toll-free 1-800 number that rang directly to our home landline.

Our family, especially my three sisters and David's sister and brother, were excited for us. But they, too, voiced some skepticism about our plan. They were worried. It was hard for them to imagine how this open adoption plan could work. We shared those fears, but never mind — into *The Book* we went.

Weeks and months passed without any calls. Matching with an expecting mother considering adoption seemed a near-impossible task. We went to monthly meetings of hopeful adoptive couples and met some wonderful people, which was helpful. All of them were waiting for that phone call from an expecting mother. We were encouraged every time we heard about couples who got a call or were successfully matched. But for all concerned, it was a slow, painful wait. We learned that it generally takes at least two years to adopt, and we needed to be patient.

***

When we decided to adopt a second time, I thought we were pros, and I knew just what to do, so I started writing our Dear birth mother letter. Jenna was excited too about a sibling for Finley, so she offered to talk to any expecting mothers on our behalf.

Despite my experience, I made some mistakes. I was worried that no one would pick us because we already had a two-year-old. I reasoned, why would an expecting mother pick a couple with a toddler when they could choose a childless couple so that their baby would be the center of attention? Consequently, I placed a picture of just David and me at the top of the page and a picture of us with Finley at the bottom. Then I wrote a letter saying what I thought an expecting mother wanted to hear. In February 1997, back in *The Book* we went.

Months passed with no calls. I knew I had to change something. Finally, I figured out that our letter was not reflecting our authentic selves. It needed to show who we were, not assume an expecting mother or father's reaction. It needed to reflect the whole of our family. And, of course, the reality was that Finley was the center of our universe — our pride and joy! I placed our picture with Finley front and center and wrote all about life with our precious child. After all, this was our authentic story. The picture portrayed fun because David was lying down on the floor propped up on his elbows with toddler Finley riding on his back, a big smile on their faces, and I was holding on to them. Once our letter reflected our true selves, things started happening. (This revised letter can be found in the appendix.)

We got a call from the Providence Place counselor a few months after our revised letter was finalized, telling us that a couple, Rachel and Ricky, were interested in meeting us. She explained that both this expecting mother and father and their families were very involved. It was unusual for the expecting father and his family to be engaged because the involvement is often mostly with the expecting mother and sometimes her mother. Rachel was fifteen, Ricky was sixteen, and they were living in Austin. They had already signed up as clients with Providence Place since Rachel's uncle had adopted from there a few years before. The counselor described them as very young and sweet dispositioned. Though they had spoken to two other couples, and Rachel's mother wanted her to choose one that was childless, they were attracted to our letter and wanted to meet us.

We were delighted when Rachel and Ricky called. By this time, we had been in *The Book* for over a year. After speaking on the phone, we agreed to go to Austin and meet them at the food court in the local mall. Importantly, we were to bring Finley with us because they wanted to meet us all together. Finley was a fundamental reason they were so drawn to us.

During our meeting, they were gracious and engaging, but we sensed that they were also stressed and nervous. Rachel was about five months pregnant. We felt an instant bond with these two, and we knew they liked us, but Rachel was particularly reticent. What struck me was how supportive they were of each other.

When I interviewed Ricky for this book, he remembered that they went to some meetings after they signed up with the adoption agency. They had a counselor, but he can't recall much about her. Mostly, he remembers flipping through *The Book* with Rachel and her mom, looking at potential adoptive parents. They picked maybe two or three couples. He remembered meeting at least one of the other couples before us but did not feel good about them. They seemed insincere to him or, at least, were not people they would get along with.

Ricky remembers seeing toddler Finley's picture and being focused on their baby having the support of a sibling. Rachel and her sisters were especially close, and they wanted their baby to have a "partner in crime" to grow up with. Ricky said, "There is wisdom behind many things in the universe, and maybe I would call it divine intervention. When we met, divine intervention spoke very clearly to Rachel and me." He said it had been an easy decision to select us.

I smile every time I hear Rachel and Ricky tell us that toddler Finley was an important part of why they were attracted to us. I think about the first letter I wrote when we decided to adopt again. I had been so worried no one would choose us because we already had a child that I downplayed our toddler. It was not until I put Finley front and center that we got the call. That was my lesson that open adoption can only work if you are truthful, authentic, and sincere.

4. The First Phone Call

"No — stay put, we will let you know when to come."

— Adoption Counselor

After several months of being in *The Book* the first time, we got a call that an expecting mother, Joann, wanted to meet with us. I was overjoyed, nervous, and shaky. My self-confidence disappeared for a moment as I contemplated that first meeting.

We happily took the three-hour drive from Houston to San Antonio to meet her at the agency, where we met not only Joann but also, to our surprise, her father. As the counselor settled us into the small room on comfortable chairs, Joann sat close to her dad on the couch for needed support. Joann said that the birth father chose not to come but did not say why. We were just thrilled that Joann wanted to interview us, and we didn't want to ask too many questions. She was far along, and the baby would arrive within two months — a baby boy. Joann was a beautiful young woman with olive skin and long, straight dark hair.

After a relatively short meeting comfortably facilitated by the counselor, Joann said she wanted to match with us, and of course, we wanted to match with her too. All we could think about was the prospect of bringing a baby home. Our letter came out of *The Book*, and we became an officially matched waiting couple.

But then, there wasn't much connection after that first meeting. Most of the contact was through the adoption counselor. I wished I could know more about Joann and wanted to talk or meet with her again, but she was in control of the relationship. I remember thinking about her father, a small statured Hispanic, more boy than man. David is half Asian and half Caucasian. I am Caucasian. What if this baby looked nothing like us? Would we love him just the same? Could he love us just the same? The world was not as open to mixed families thirty years ago as it is today, and deep down, I was wondering how open I could be.

I pushed all those thoughts aside, and we got the nursery ready. It was so much fun picking out a crib, clothes, and room decorations. We visited Babies R Us and other local baby stores to see the latest trends in baby furniture and décor. There were so many new baby gadgets to choose from. We were in awe of items from angled bottle nipples to battery powered swings. And I read those articles on the merits of powdered baby formula over breast milk — perfect. What a fun time we had dreaming about bringing a baby home. We chose bright blues, pinks, yellows, and greens. Not the traditional pastels because we had read that a baby prefers bright colors. It was a cheerful room. We were ready!

The call finally came that Joann was in labor. We told our counselor we could be there in four hours. But she said, "No — stay put, we will let you know when to come." How disappointing and confusing. Once the baby was born, she called and told us that Joann was having second thoughts, and they were going to place the baby with foster parents to give her time to decide. The baby was placed in the care of a wonderful couple, whom we never met, but the foster mom called me every day for a week and gave me a report on the baby I had wanted so badly to adopt. But alas, just over one week after he was born, Joann did change her mind and took the baby home. We were crushed, but we knew in our hearts that it was the best decision for Joann and the baby, and we were grateful that we had never held that child.

5. Leap of Faith

"Three things are important to us: that you would be capable parents, that you love each other, and that we can trust you."

— Jenna, expecting mother

After our difficult experience with Joann, back in *The Book* we went, waiting and waiting for another call. Months passed, and one did indeed come — but from a very unexpected place.

It had been nearly a year since we became an official waiting couple for the first time. Over the short span of the next twelve days, what happened was thrilling, intense, and an emotional roller-coaster ride.

I was sitting at my desk that Tuesday afternoon, trying to do a thousand things at once. I had a call on hold, one on the line, a stack of mail, an even larger email backlog, and I was preparing to facilitate a seminar. I was under a lot of stress when my assistant walked in and handed me a note that my friend Eva was on the line. I said I would call her back. But then I got hold of myself, quickly realizing that a call from Eva might be important. Eva and her husband were another waiting couple also going through the process, and we had become friends. It took me about two minutes to drop everything and call her back.

Eva explained that they had just matched with an expecting mother, and then they got a call from a friend of a friend who knew another expecting mother. They asked us if we would mind if they sent her our letter. Would we mind? Of course not! Please do. And that is how we met Jenna and Michael — Finley's birth parents.

Jenna's best friend at the time was Parker. Parker's mother was friends with Eva, and hence the connection was made. When our letter landed in Jenna's hands, she was trying to make an appointment with Planned Parenthood to schedule an abortion. We will never know what would have happened had our letter not been given to Jenna, but there is no doubt in my mind that divine intervention was at work.

Eva paved the way and Jenna called me that very night. A sweet voice on the other end of the phone sounded relieved. She shared a lot with me that first night. She had just turned seventeen, was in high school, and living with a high school friend and his single mom. But now, with news of the pregnancy, her friend's mom had asked her to move out. Jenna's mom had fallen on hard times and could not support her, so she wasn't sure if she could move in with her. Jenna had had no contact with her father for the last couple of years. At only eight weeks pregnant, she and Michael thought that abortion was the best solution, but when Jenna thought about that, she couldn't sleep.

After learning that there was something called open adoption, she felt that was a better solution; with that possibility, she was now sleeping better. Jenna listened while I explained how the process worked and then she agreed to contact our adoption counselor the next day.

After speaking with the counselor, Jenna called me and said she and Michael wanted to meet us on Saturday. It was all happening so fast. We were so excited, and they lived in Houston, too, so it would be an easy drive. Jenna gave us an address, and we were to meet at the apartment of Michael's older brother.

We arrived at the large, sprawling apartment complex typical of Houston, and after some difficulty finding the right unit, we climbed the stairs to the second-floor apartment. We were nervous, and our hearts were beating fast as we knocked on the door.

In a moment, the most beautiful girl with brown hair in a pixie cut, sparkling eyes, and a nervous smile opened the door. She wore blue jeans and a plaid flannel shirt, and I instantly loved her. Then Michael, a darling teen boy, appeared. After anxious smiles and awkward greetings, we piled into our car to drive to the restaurant for our first meeting.

We went to Fuddruckers, a perfect spot for teenagers. It was a popular hamburger restaurant with rolls of paper towels at each table, a promise of a large messy burger served in a basket lined with paper and stuffed with oversized fries. After ordering at the counter, they gave us large cups, and we each helped ourselves to the soda fountain and settled in at a table to wait for our food. Instantly, David spilled his entire Texas-sized soda…and then Jenna did too. We were all so nervous, but we laughed about that many times afterward.

Jenna and Michael captured our hearts immediately. They were so scared and so brave at the same time. They held hands, and we began to talk, explaining what open adoption was and why we thought openness was good. We would pause to ask if they had questions, but they told us to just keep talking. Michael said he thought he would have so many questions, but they did not come to mind.

Jenna shared that she had told her mom about the pregnancy the previous night. She was so relieved when her mom hugged her and told her that she loved her. That meant a lot. Jenna's mom offered to find a way for her to move in and said that her door was always open. She knew her mom was having a difficult time and was relieved.

Michael was sincere and seemed mature for a teen. He was trying to keep a positive perspective. "It's not like Jenna or me are dying," he said. "We can get through this." Michael shared that he had a twin brother who lived with his mom in Alabama. His parents were divorced. He was supposed to move to Alabama too, but he did not want to leave Jenna, so he was living with his father, who did not yet know about the pregnancy.

Michael and Jenna attended different high schools but still saw each other on the weekends. When Michael started to tell us more, he hesitated. It was clear that life for these two was difficult, and Michael wasn't sure how long he could stay in Texas before going to Alabama.

Jenna also shared that she had not seen a doctor yet, and we encouraged her to speak to the adoption counselor, who could help her with medical issues and expenses.

Once a match takes place, the agency can help an expecting mother with expenses such as rent, medical, food, hygiene, etc. She sends receipts to the adoption agency, which then bills the waiting adoptive parents. There is, of course, no guarantee of placement and no refunds if the adoption plan does not go through, but that was the last thing on our minds. The most important thing was to do everything by the rules, and through the agency since there cannot be any implication of payment in exchange for a placement.

Also, during this first meeting, we felt obligated to tell Jenna and Michael that the adoption agency had a book full of waiting couples. While we secretly hoped they would not want to look further for options, we knew they needed to have all the information. And if they ultimately wanted to match and place with us, it would be for all the right reasons.

During our drive back to the apartment, David and Michael talked about cars. The conversation flowed naturally and easily. We also told them that they could set the pace for communication. Jenna promised to call our counselor on Monday, and as we said good-bye, I hugged Jenna, and she hugged me back tight. David hugged Jenna too. I took both of Michael's hands in mine with a warm squeeze to say good-bye, then he and David shook hands, and we drove away. We were not even out of the apartment complex when we looked at each other and said, "Yes! Yes! Yes! Seven months is a long wait, but these two are worth it."

First thing Monday morning, we spoke with our counselor to confirm that we would be interested in a match with Jenna and Michael. Fortunately, after a few more days, Jenna called the agency too about the next steps, and the counselor agreed to meet at Jenna's high school the following week. Jenna needed to apply to work with Providence Place and sign an affidavit that Michael was the father. The agency needed to determine if Jenna had any medical insurance coverage. They also required a doctor's report to confirm the pregnancy and an address of where Jenna would be living. Jenna had the option of living at Providence Place but preferred to live with her mother. In this case, her mother's household income determined how much financial support Jenna would receive.

We were not worried about any of these things. All we needed was word that Jenna and Michael were interested in matching with us, though we would have to wait for that.

In the meantime, as fate would have it, Michael's older brother happened to be tinting windows in the downtown office building where we both worked. That same week, we went to the floor where he was working to meet him. Michael's brother paused his work and was genuine, friendly, and open to meeting us. He thought Jenna and Michael were making a good decision about adoption. His girlfriend had been pregnant at nineteen, and they married and were raising their son. Although he was tinting windows for now, they both wanted to go to college. It was hard raising a child. He also said his father did not yet know about the pregnancy, but he was sure that both Michael's father and mother would support an adoption plan. He told us Michael had always been the baby of the family — even as a twin, he was always the smaller one. Michael's brother vowed to help them in any way he could, and we could tell that he believed adoption was the best plan for his little brother. We parted, feeling one step closer but also wondering if we would ever meet again.

When I got home from work, there was a message on our recorder. It was from Diane, an expecting mother living not too far from us. She had seen our letter in the Providence Place book and wanted us to call her back.

We didn't know what to do — another expecting mother. After all, we were not yet matched with Jenna and Michael (except in our hearts), and Jenna had not even signed up yet as a Providence Place client. We didn't even know if Jenna and Michael wanted to meet other couples. We called our counselor, and she advised us to talk to Diane and that it was best to keep all options open.

I said a prayer, called Diane, and got her voice mail. I called a second time the next day and left another message explaining that we would be going for a bike ride Saturday morning but would be home by 1:00 p.m.

We biked forty-five miles that Saturday and came home exhausted. But sure enough, when we returned, there was a message on our phone. However, it wasn't

Jenna, and it wasn't Diane. It was Ruth — *another* expecting mother. Again, I said a prayer and called Ruth back.

Ruth said that she had been crying a lot, so if she cried while we were talking, not to be alarmed. For over an hour, she talked, and I listened. She was eighteen years old and having a baby girl in thirteen weeks and one day. After reading fifty adoptive parent letters from several agencies, she thought about it deeply and chose us. Our letter had caught her attention — the bear and circle picture especially. There had been another family she was considering, but they had a nine-year-old boy, and Ruth was afraid that the boy would someday say that he was the real child, not her daughter.

Ruth shared so much. Physically, she felt fine but tired easily. She wanted her baby to have more than she did, and she was not in school but planned to get her GED. In high school, she had gotten mixed up with the wrong crowd and could not go back to school with those former friends.

Ruth's parents were supportive, but she was living with a friend. Her mom lived close by and called her three times a week, but they argued too much. Since she could not come and go as she pleased, she could not live with parents; she needed her freedom. The friend she lived with had a fourteen-month-old baby, and Ruth often held her, fed her, and sat with her. She knew how hard it was to take care of a baby and did not want to be selfish with her own child.

Her mom supported her adoption decision fully now. When Ruth was only five weeks pregnant, her mom advised her to have an abortion. They had fought about it, but Ruth was stubborn and wanted to prove to her mother that she could take care of this baby. Then her mom suggested adoption, which Ruth also refused. But one day, she didn't know why, she started listening to her mom, and it made sense.

She even told me about her hospital plans in that very first phone call. When the baby was born, she wanted to be moved off the maternity floor right away and did not want to see her. She felt that she could handle pictures but nothing more. Further, she thought that when her daughter turned eighteen, she could look Ruth up if she wanted to. And that was why open adoption appealed to her.

Her biggest fear about open adoption was that when her daughter became a teenager, she might ask to live with Ruth. She said that since she herself was a rotten teen, she would not want that, so it worried her.

Then Ruth told me about the birth father. She could not find him and only knew his first name. When she had asked if he was ready to be a dad, he split. She said he would not be a problem. (Of course, I knew that not getting an expecting father to relinquish could be a big problem.) She only had one picture of him, but said he was a six-foot-two-inch-tall body builder, weighed 215 pounds, and had carrot-red hair and blue eyes. Ruth was five feet three inches tall with brown hair and eyes and had big bones, hips, and bust. She saw a doctor regularly, took all her prenatal vitamins, and had kept all the sonogram reports for us to see.

Ruth enjoyed mostly English in school, worked on the school paper, and was part of the drama club and yearbook. She wrote short stories, and her mom thought she should have them published.

By the time our conversation ended, I was anxious and exhausted. Ruth sounded sincere, but I knew she needed good counseling and had much to work out. I told her we would be in touch. I did share with her that we were not matched yet, but that we were talking to other expecting mothers so that she would know. She was honest and vulnerable, and my heart ached for her. This was much harder than I thought it would be.

David and I were not sure what to do about Diane and Ruth. We did not want to meet with them if Jenna and Michael wanted to match. So, I called Jenna to tell her that we had some other calls from expecting mothers, but the last thing I wanted was for her to feel pressure. She said she understood perfectly and did not mind my call. She and Michael had decided that they did not want to interview other couples. Jenna said, "Three things are important to us: that you would be capable parents, that you love each other, and that we can trust you." Since they felt we met all three criteria, they wanted to move forward with us. I thought, *Wow, that's profound thinking for these young teens.* We were so impressed and grateful.

Jenna further said that all the questions and issues around childrearing were unimportant. She and Michael felt that we would do a better job of parenting than they could. She went on to say that she planned to call the adoption counselor on Monday to confirm. What a relief.

About an hour later, Diane called. We had a short honest conversation. I wanted to reach through the phone and hug her, but I had to tell her my heart was with Jenna and Michael. I later learned that Diane had her baby that July and placed with another waiting couple from our agency. I had just a twinge of doubt and regret, thinking that it could have been us and, of course, hoping and praying that everything would work out with Jenna and Michael. I never found out what Ruth ended up deciding.

That marked the end of twelve days I will never forget, and the beginning of our lifetime journey with Jenna and Michael.

***

During our second adoption, we were in *The Book* for fifteen months before we met our match with Rachel and Ricky. Once again, we were fortunate enough to speak to other expecting mothers too.

Our first call came from the mother of a pregnant girl. She was obviously concerned for and loved her daughter very much. After two or three phone calls with the girl's mom, we felt something wasn't right, and we weren't sure if we could trust her. She did not seem to want us to meet or even talk to her daughter. And then she started to push, almost wanting us to make commitments over the phone. After a few more uncomfortable phone calls, we decided to end the discussion, and I recall the grandmother being upset with us. Later, we learned that the girl was mentally disabled and probably incapable of making her own decisions. Her mother had not told us about this situation, but our instincts were correct that she had not been upfront with us. We were sympathetic to her situation, but if we were to be honest, we would not have matched knowing about these challenges.

A few months later we got another call from an expecting mother. We spoke several times and developed a relationship over the phone. We had a good rapport and I thought things were going well when we made plans for our first face-to-face meeting. But I got a surprise call from her mom the night before the planned meeting. She canceled our meeting and told me the family was not supportive of an adoption plan. I never heard from her again. That was my first lesson on the importance of the grandmother. In retrospect, I realize that if an expecting mother has the help and support of her own mother, no matter her final decision, she is blessed. So often, these women do not have the mothers they desperately need.

These interactions took a real emotional toll on us. But we were undeterred.

About the time we first met with Rachel and Ricky but were not yet matched, we got a call from the Providence Place counselor about another expecting mother who was interested in meeting us. Her name was Kylie. The counselor described Kylie as beautiful and likable. She was also raising a blond, blue-eyed two-year-old son. Since Kylie had experience caring for a child, she knew how hard it was and felt that she just could not do it again. We were her first choice, but she had also picked second and third-choice potential parents.

The counselor then went on to say that she was a bright girl; however, she was currently in jail for unauthorized use of a vehicle. Kylie had told the agency it was a total misunderstanding, and she would be getting out of jail very soon. She also shared that Kylie had been dancing at a topless bar in Austin before her arrest. The father was someone she hung out with at the bar, and she was pretty sure she could find him. We learned that while she had experimented with drugs in the past, she had not used any during her pregnancy. It was a lot of information to take in, and we were skeptical. But we did not automatically assume that a match with her could not work. We remained open to all possibilities.

A few days later, the counselor called to say that she had met with Kylie the previous day, and she was now out of jail. Kylie had found religion and wanted to do things right. She again confirmed that Kylie had not used any illegal drugs during her pregnancy and reported that Kylie's mother had looked after Kylie's son during her jail time. She was still considering three couples, and she was likely to call us that night. The counselor then encouraged us to meet with her.

We traveled to Austin to meet Kylie at a McDonald's the next weekend. She was due in just a few weeks, and her adorable, curly blond-headed two-year-old son was with her. She told us she just could not take care of another child and wanted to make an adoption plan. I must admit that I could not help but notice her stunning thick strawberry red hair. We had a cordial meeting, answered all of her questions about our families, and agreed that we would be in touch soon.

As we were driving home, something bothered me. I did not trust her. It was an instinct more than anything else because we liked her quite a bit. I remember calling the counselor and asking how important trust was, and she told me that in an open adoption, you must have it. Without it, you are setting yourself up for problems. Still, it was hard to let go of a potential match. They were so hard to get, and our clocks were ticking. Kylie had declared that she wanted to match with us, but our hearts were with Rachel and Ricky. We decided to wait and hoped they felt the same way about us.

Later, we learned that Kylie had placed her baby with a couple and then changed her mind. I never found out anything else, but we were grateful to have been spared the heartbreak both Kylie and the adoptive parents must have felt.

At this point you might be thinking — *how on earth did we connect with so many expecting mothers considering adoption?* During the early 90's there were many more expecting parents considering adoption than there are in 2024. (The decrease in numbers is driven by better access to birth control, abortion, and social services for single parents who choose to raise the child.) Also, at that time, expecting mothers were encouraged by the agency to contact prospective adoptive parents directly (this is no longer a best practice). Finally, our Dear birth mother letter was unique — we were one of the first to use fun colors and artwork that resonated with young mothers — and that attracted positive attention.

6. Matched Again

"It is important to remember that this agreement is based on trust, mutual caring, and respect between birth parents and adoptive parents."

— Excerpt from first six-month cooperative agreement

The day after Jenna told us that she and Michael did not want to interview other couples, our adoption counselor went to Jenna's school to meet with Jenna and her mom, Susan. That day, Jenna signed the papers to become a Providence Place client. We knew it was good for Jenna to have her mom by her side as she made that decision.

Jenna called me the next day to tell me about her meeting with the adoption counselor and wondered if we could meet her mother the following weekend. We were more than thrilled at the prospect of meeting Susan.

As the weekend approached, Jenna had not called to confirm the time and place. I was getting very anxious now. It is hard to describe how desperately we wanted things to work out, but at the same time, how important it was for Jenna to be in control, to set the pace, and make the decisions that were best for her. However, it was more than I could stand, so by Sunday, I called Jenna, who sounded as if she had been expecting my call. She immediately apologized for not getting back to me and explained that she had arrived home late from Galveston the night before, and even though she'd set the alarm to call me in the morning, she had slept through it. (How many times had my teen children done the exact same thing — sleeping through alarms.) She said her mom was not feeling well, and we would need to meet another day. Of course, that was not a problem, and I told her we had plenty of time. Jenna shared that she was feeling good — no nausea or morning sickness. And she confirmed that her father's insurance would cover some of her medical bills. Nice news.

Over the following weeks, I had several phone calls with Jenna. She talked about the baby, her doctor's appointments, and how she felt physically. She was reading her mom's nursing books to learn about pregnancy. Jenna was unhappy about Michael's plans to move to Alabama over the summer, but she knew he needed to be with his mother and twin brother. As long as he returned for the baby's birth, she was ok because she figured she would need him more then. Michael had definitely been getting the brunt of her mood swings, but she quickly added that she had good days too. We knew we needed to promptly set a date for an official match meeting before Michael left.

Jenna called and suggested that we all meet at her mom's apartment. The plan was for us to pick up Michael from his high school on Friday and bring him to the apartment for a 4:00 p.m. meeting. Our adoption counselor would meet us there to facilitate the match.

Jenna thought maybe she was farther along than she initially figured but would be going to the doctor soon. She said people were telling her she looked more like five months along than three months, and she could no longer wear her jeans, so she wore mostly sundresses. Her friend had gifted her the first maternity dress and soon she would need to add to her maternity wardrobe. Luckily, she had found a box with clothes that used to be too big for her that she could now wear. Blue jeans were a staple, and happily, there were some baggy-cut jeans in that box.

Jenna also shared that she had been having some cramps and pressure pains but had read in one of her mom's books that the baby is undergoing rapid growth in the fifth month, so that could explain her discomfort.

Jenna was especially excited on that day because her sister, who was currently living with their dad, was planning to move back to Houston if their mom landed a new job. Jenna's sister had visited the previous weekend, and it had been wonderful for both of them because her sister was her best friend.

She asked that we call Michael to get directions to his school for the Friday match meeting. When we called, Michael answered but quickly asked that we speak to his dad to get directions. That was our first contact with Michael's dad, and we took the opportunity to express how much we appreciated his support of Michael in the adoption decision. He said he felt it was the right decision as Michael was so young and deserved an education. He did not want the children — Jenna and Michael — to suffer over this. Although he did not ask us any questions, he shared that both Michael and his oldest son had good things to say about us. We agreed that perhaps one day we would meet each other. He then gave us directions and his work phone number in case we had any trouble finding the school.

Nearly two months after our first meeting, the official match day was set. David and I both took vacation days. The night before, we went to a Phil Collins concert, but I did not enjoy it much because all I could think of was our match meeting.

Everything went exactly as planned. We picked Michael up at school and had an easy chat on the way to Jenna's. I could tell that Michael trusted and looked up to David. He asked David about college and if it was hard. Michael was thinking about getting a business degree, but first, he wanted to earn some money. He talked about moving to Alabama for the summer.

We pulled into Jenna's apartment complex at the same time as our adoption counselor. Jenna and Susan were waiting, and we all hugged hello. This was the first time we were to meet Jenna's mom and the first time for our adoption counselor to meet Michael. We entered the small apartment, and it took a few awkward moments to figure out who would sit where. Finally, we settled in for the marathon match meeting. I thought Susan was pretty, and it struck me that day that even Jenna's mom, the grandmother, was my age or maybe even younger.

Jenna started with a good report from her latest doctor's visit. The counselor then explained that the meeting would be in three parts: Family Background, Medical History, and Financial Support. We learned all about their families and relatives. And between them, we heard about family members with cancer, strokes, heart attacks, chronic obstructive pulmonary disease, emphysema, asthma, mental breakdowns, manic depression, alcoholism, and drug use. It was overwhelming, but we reasoned that many of these ailments would show up if you looked into any family history. We also figured that we had the resources to deal with whatever problems might arise and were undeterred and happy to have the information.

Susan shared that she had been hospitalized for severe depression for fourteen months when Jenna was about five years old. After she got out of the hospital, she went to nursing school and was currently working at a hospital providing mental health care for children, where she was able to work mostly weekend night shifts. She explained that she was financially constrained and could not be much help raising Jenna's baby.

We thought Susan was positive about this adoption, but we were unsure. We did know that Jenna had not been living with her for most of her growing-up years. Susan told us that she might have some Choctaw Indian in her background, which was big news, because if a child with a Native American bloodline is placed for adoption, the Native Americans have first rights to the child. More investigation would be needed, and, fortunately, our adoption agency would do that legal work.

Jenna told us how proud she was of her pastel drawings and wanted us to see them. Her art took my breath away. It was fabulous! She had drawn a pastel chalk picture of herself and her sister that was so lifelike and beautiful. I was impressed with her talent and hoped that the baby would inherit it. (Finley did.)

Then Susan pulled out a photo album and proudly shared it. We had fun looking at her family photos, and I was touched when she gave me one of Jenna and her sister as toddlers.

After our long afternoon match meeting with the counselor, Jenna, Michael, and Susan, we were starving, so the six of us went to dinner. Our counselor was an expert at bringing up the right questions. She gave Jenna and Michael each a book to fill out for the baby with things like their favorite books, colors, food, and anything they wanted the baby to know. And when we learned over dinner that Michael planned to leave for Alabama the very next weekend, our counselor immediately went into action. She asked him if he would be willing to sign relin-

quishment papers right then and there. Normally, she would never ask for a signature during a first meeting, but by Texas law, the father could sign before the
baby is born. Our counselor knew from experience that once Michael was gone, if
we did not have a signature, it could be difficult to get it afterward. Without both
a mother's and father's signature, the legalities of adoption could become very
complex.

Our counselor went to her car trunk to get the papers and then took Michael
to a separate table where he read every word. We needed two independent wit-
nesses, so David asked two restaurant employees to step in. Michael signed without
hesitation, and the papers were witnessed. Our counselor then made plans to meet
Jenna and Michael in another couple of days to collect the books for the baby.

During that dinner, we also talked to Jenna about going back to high school in
August, recognizing that she would be seven months pregnant. Jenna wanted to
go back and thought she could do it. She knew she would not be the only one at
school who would be pregnant and felt she had enough support from her friends
and the school counselor. I can only imagine how hard it would be for any young
girl to go to high school while pregnant, but Jenna was brave and confident.

We talked about the birth, and our counselor asked Jenna if she had thought
about who she wanted in the birthing room. Jenna said she just wanted Michael
in the room, not us, but would make the final decision later. However, she said it
would be fine for us to be at the hospital. This was not a surprise since we had no
expectations about being in the birthing room and were thrilled at the prospect of
simply waiting nearby. I recognize that both of my children's birth mothers were
fortunate that their own mothers and the babies' fathers were with them for the
birth.

Jenna also said that she liked the pace of our relationship — seeing each other
monthly and talking on the phone. After the baby was born, she thought she might
just want pictures twice a year (birthday and Christmas) and no visitation, but she
was unsure. Michael said he wanted to see the baby as an infant only, then maybe
at three or four years old. His thinking was that once the baby was an adult, they

could decide about visits. Both of them wanted to be sure we could always get in touch with each other.

After a long, enjoyable, and emotional match meeting, David and I went home and slept soundly.

Three days later, our counselor called to verify that a match had been made. (She had to hear from each of us separately after the match meeting.) Done! By this time, we expected that Jenna and Michael would want to match with us, but I must admit that getting the official word was a big relief. We soon learned that the Choctaw Indians had confirmed there were no records of Jenna's family and would not intervene. More good news.

So, we began the next five-month phase of our journey together. We spoke to Jenna on the phone frequently and met occasionally. I was all consumed with looking forward to the next opportunity to connect with Jenna. I remember wanting to take her under my wing, and to this day, I can still hear her sweet laugh and see her beautiful young face in my mind.

Even though Jenna was living with Susan, we did not spend any time with this grandmother again until after Finley was born.

The same week as our match meeting in early June, both Jenna and Michael had their last school day. They had finished finals, and our counselor met with them for an afternoon session. They were in good spirits, and both had filled out the baby's keepsake books. We had been talking about names, and *Parker* kept coming to the top of our list for boy or girl. Jenna was fond of that choice because her friend Parker had brought us together. In the end, we chose Parker for the baby's middle name.

Michael left for Alabama as soon as school was over. I knew this would be a hard day for Jenna, so I called her to see how she was doing. I was relieved that she was upbeat and talked about her upcoming doctor's appointment.

A week later, Jenna called me around 9:15 p.m., and we talked for a long time. She said the doctor's appointment had been quick and easy. An ultrasound had been scheduled for Friday, and she would bring a videotape and make a copy for us.

She had felt the baby move last night for the first time and called Michael to tell him in the middle of the night, which was neat. She had expected to feel fluttering, but instead, it was more like kicking. Jenna reported that all her tests had come out just fine. No signs of spina bifida, Down's syndrome, or diabetes. Her iron was low, so she got supplements for that and said they were helping with her energy level. She also started taking over-the-counter vitamins.

Jenna was happy to report that Michael was settling well in Alabama so far and had started to work out because he was getting a belly and wanted to get rid of it. They decided to go to both their proms next year — hers in Texas and his in Alabama. She figured that he would be in Texas for the first school semester but back in Alabama for the second one. They planned to do the entire thing for one prom — dinner out and pictures. For the second prom, they would just go to the dance, and Jenna could wear the same dress since it would be different friend groups. Sadly, they broke up and did not make either prom as a couple.

Jenna also shared that she had been thinking a lot about a career in graphic arts instead of teaching. She had already talked to her teacher about him helping her with scholarships and industry contacts (she was his favorite student) and had her eye on a school in Waco.

That night, Jenna talked to David on the phone too. I could tell they were having fun discussing bike adventures. David told Jenna that we loved her.

We closed by making plans for her to see the house in a couple of weeks. She said that she was ready to see the baby's room. She told me she was excited for us and thought we deserved to be the parents of her baby. She expressed that she did not know how other mothers felt, but she was happy for us. Hearing this from Jenna made my heart soar. I realize now that Jenna was feeling comfortable with us, and I think she was trying her best to make everyone — including herself — feel good and right about the adoption plan. She promised to call on Friday after the sonogram to tell us the sex of the baby. I remember wanting to wait to hear the news face-to-face.

Jenna called to say the sonogram went well, but the baby was positioned such that they could not tell if it was a boy or a girl because the baby was in a breech position, knees up, legs crossed behind the back with the umbilical cord in between the legs. Before the sonogram, she had to drink lots of water — not just a couple of glasses but the jumbo things you get at the Stop-n-Go. We laughed about how hard that was. She also reported that she could see five fingers and five toes. I could not get enough of these details. It was such a privilege that Jenna wanted to share them all with me. She would return in two weeks for another sonogram.

Just as things were smoothly moving along, our counselor called to inform us that she was leaving and that we would be getting a new adoption counselor in July. I was most concerned for Jenna since she seemed to be doing well with her counseling sessions. However, we were assured that the new counselor was experienced, and the transition would be seamless.

She also suggested I gather any books Jenna had written down as favorites to keep as a special gift to the baby. Jenna's favorite book was *The Secret Garden*, and I think I collected about three different versions of that for Finley. *Anything to keep the connection*, I thought.

Jenna was looking forward to visiting our home but was disappointed that her mom could not make it. She planned to bring Parker instead. I thought it would be good to meet Jenna's close friend. It was a little challenging to coordinate all our schedules, but we finally agreed on a Saturday in early July.

We were to pick up Jenna and Parker at Susan's apartment, go out to breakfast, and then take Parker home since she had to work that afternoon. Jenna ended up coming to see our home alone.

When we arrived at the apartment, we were greeted by Jenna, Susan, Parker, and Susan's new golden retriever puppy. After exchanging some pleasantries, David and I took off with Jenna and Parker to La Madeleine, a breakfast restaurant, and we went awkwardly through the ordering line — all of us a little nervous.

Finally, we sat down and relaxed. The girls mostly talked about college and their hopeful choices. Jenna was having second thoughts about that technical school in Waco and was now hoping to go to a bigger school like Parker, who wanted to study the environment and biology. They were, in every sense, typical teens.

A colleague of ours happened to be at the restaurant, and he and his wife came over to say hello. We made some introductions and exchanged conversation for a few cordial moments before they were on their way. This was one of those times where you think, *How do I handle this?* We probably introduced the girls as friends because the next day at work, my coworker asked who they were. However, he had been one of the recipients of our "Dear birth mother" letter and had suspected Jenna or Parker might be expecting. He was surprised at their youth and, of course, was inquisitive about the process.

This type of encounter is something we did not plan for. There are upsides and downsides to sending letters to family, friends, and colleagues to announce that you are looking to connect with someone wanting to make an adoption plan. People are genuine and supportive but curious above all. We have learned that we did not need to explain our relationship with Jenna to everyone. Sometimes it was fine just to introduce her as a friend. There is a time and place for everything, and Jenna deserved privacy.

On the walk from the restaurant to the car, I couldn't help but notice how beautiful Jenna looked in her blue, white, and yellow flowered dress. Standing up, she looked quite pregnant now, and she proudly let me feel her belly right there in the parking lot. I was so grateful to Jenna that she shared this intimate moment with me, and I have carried that memory with me ever since.

On the drive back to Parker's house, I enjoyed listening to the girls' chat in the back seat. They talked about summer jobs and boys, particularly focusing on one very cute but very stuck-up boy. They giggled and said, "So many boys... so little time."

As we approached Parker's house, her little white poodle ran up to greet us, and her mother came out too. She was our connection to Jenna, and we were grateful to have met her. We chatted for a few moments in the driveway, then said our good-byes and left to take Jenna to our home.

It was a long forty-five-minute drive, and I needlessly worried about everything. Would we have enough to talk about? What would Jenna think of our neighborhood? It was a transition area close to downtown with a range of homes from tiny rundown bungalows to large two-story brick new builds. Our street was mixed. Would this bother Jenna? What would she think when she walked into our home? Did it look like a home for her baby? How would she feel when she saw the nursery? Would it upset her or make her happy? My mind would not stop churning.

I was in the front passenger seat, and Jenna was in the back, so I had to turn my head and strain to see her. To my delight, she talked for the entire drive. She filled us in on the events that had led to her current living situation and why she had been disconnected from her father for the last two years. We were in such uncharted territory, getting to know each other without any clear vision of the future, and I became obsessed with soaking up every detail.

Jenna explained that she had lived with her dad and stepmother most of her life, along with her younger sister and her stepsister, who was the same age as Jenna. I am guessing that she went to live with her dad when her mother was hospitalized for severe depression. She was very close to her sister but not to her stepsister. It had not been a harmonious household, especially for the last two or three years she had lived there. Her stepmother was not a bad person, she explained, but had a lot of problems. She was depressed, and it had gotten worse as the years went by, especially when her father was not at home. His work in the oil production business took him away for weeks at a time.

Jenna was a good kid who stayed in her room most of the time reading, but she was the black sheep of the family. She was pretty vocal and always stood up to her father when he had disagreements with her stepmother and siblings. Both her stepmother and stepsister resented her for this. At times feisty with family members, she admitted that once she took a position, she stubbornly stuck to it no matter what. In retrospect, she thought maybe she deserved some of their reactions.

When I think about Finley, they had the exact same behavior as a young teen. Once they made up their mind or took a position, there was no backing down or talking them out of it. Finley was often stubborn and stuck to their position at all costs. *Could this be genetic?*

Finally, we arrived home. Jenna looked around and smiled. She said that our counselor had told her everything matched in our house — even the purple crepe myrtle trees outside our kitchen window matched our purple and green ceramic dishes.

We gave her the tour, starting in our backyard, where we had a small patio and fenced-in yard — perfect for a sandbox. After walking through the living and dining rooms, we sat down and chatted in my favorite room, the study. Jenna told us about how she had used the paintbox feature on the school's computer to paint a horse and had spent hours zooming in and filling in all the details with different colors. She was so proud of that work. She talked about how she and her sister played computer games on her father's computer. Her sister was into Nintendo, but Jenna loved the strategy games just like David. Then David and Jenna got into a discussion about computer games, and I got lost listening to the lingo, but it was a sweet bonding moment for them.

David retreated to the kitchen while I took Jenna upstairs to see the nursery. When she walked into the baby's room, her eyes lit up, and she smiled. I was so relieved. She loved the bright colors, suitable for a boy or a girl. The crib was set up on one side, and a single bed sat in the other corner, along with a rocking chair and ottoman. A dresser doubled as a changing table. Jenna sat on the rocker, and I sat on the bed, and we talked for a long while, just the two of us.

Jenna talked about the baby and how he kept her awake. We did not know the sex yet, but she referred to the baby as he and said that just when she was ready to fall asleep, he got active. It was a gentle flutter and did not hurt, but it would not let her sleep. She said it was like that pulse in your arm from a nerve, only bigger. It was hard to tell if it was a kick or a fist, but she sure felt it, and she was happy.

Jenna then changed the subject, going on to share details about the boy she had dated before Michael. This boy was not good to her — he had been very critical and did a lot to tear down her self-esteem. Before him, she had been outgoing and enjoyed meeting people. But he had changed her. He was smart, had even skipped a grade, and was good-looking and full of himself. She wasn't sure why she had fallen for him, and after they broke up, he talked badly about her. Then, she started to cry. I wanted to hug or touch her but didn't because I sensed she needed space. Instead, I handed her a teddy bear from the crib, and she hugged it. I took a stuffed bunny and sat on the floor closer to her while we continued to talk.

When I think of that time with Jenna, I recognize that Finley and Jenna are similar in needing their own space and shying away from physical affection. Even as a young child, Finley never wanted to be comforted with a touch or a hug. Perhaps Finley got that from Jenna. Or, as I learned much later, it is not unusual for an adopted child to be unable to accept their mother's affection. Instead, they keep a distance in an effort to feel less vulnerable.

Michael, she explained, had helped her through some tough times. However, both were realistic about their relationship and had decided that even if it did not work out, they would always remain friends.

The subject then turned to spirituality. I said I was not sure about many things, but I thought that we, as humans, are more spiritual than physical. She agreed, noting that she was still developing her thoughts about God and someday might want to join a church. Her father's family was Methodist, and there were even some preachers in the group. But her father rejected the religion and hadn't raised her in a church. She was interested in universal consciousness but wasn't sure what to believe. However, she was happy that we intended to raise the baby in a church community, no matter what denomination.

David then came to find us since we had been gone so long. During dinner, Jenna was excited to tell us that she had a summer job working four hours a day caring for a single mom's three children, ages five to eleven. She explained how important it was for her to work and stay busy.

For dessert, I made a lemon cake with chocolate icing because I had read in the book that Jenna prepared for the baby that this was her favorite. Of course, I wanted to please her. All too soon, it was time to take Jenna home. During the easy, comfortable ride, Jenna talked about her days as a breaststroker on the swim team, how she had practiced every day and competed in meets on Saturdays. Her parents never came to watch her meets, but she understood because it was always so long, hot, and boring. Her favorite part was watching the little kids as they swam and then had to stop and hold on to the ropes. She also complained about the cliques at school and how hard it was to understand high school girls, which was why she kept to her close friends. I promised her that it would get easier when high school was over.

Before we knew it, we were walking her to the steps leading up to her apartment. We did not attempt to go in or see Susan since it had been a long, emotional day for all of us. After some good-bye hugs, she promised to let us know the results of her next doctor's appointment.

The following week, Jenna put me in touch with her doctor. The doctor gave me an update, and we talked about prenatal vitamins. I was concerned because Michael had shared that he had experimented with drugs, and I was worried about how this might affect the baby. But Jenna's doctor eased our concerns. This must have also been when Jenna found out the sex of the baby, but I do not recall the moment we learned that happy news.

Eventually, we decided on the name Finley Parker. Jenna was good with that choice too and wanted it to be our decision. We chose Finley simply because we liked the name. We had thought deeply about naming the baby after our mothers or other relatives, but since this was an adoption, we did not want to favor our family or Jenna's family over the other, so we just picked a name that made us smile. And, of course, we had chosen Parker because it had a connection to Jenna.

Thankfully, the change in adoption counselors was seamless as promised. Jenna went to Alabama to visit Michael, which I think helped her tremendously. It had been a long, lonely summer for her.

7. Raistlin

"I just can't raise another baby at this point in my life."

— Kim, birth grandmother

By August, Jenna had gone back to high school but was clearly struggling. We continued to talk on the phone often, and while she remained upbeat, she had concerns. Our discussions included everything from math class struggles to her relationships with her mom, dad, sister, stepmom, and stepsister. It was a hard time in her life — not only because of the pregnancy but because she was a teen and moving in with a mom who was often absent. With Michael in Alabama, life was stressful and lonely.

Finally, October arrived. The baby was due in one month, so our counselor facilitated a meeting between Jenna, David, and me to create a cooperative agreement that would outline our expectations for the next six months. The agreement was a form with questions, and I hand wrote Jenna's responses. It was not a legal agreement, but the discussion helped tremendously. The meeting was not difficult, and Jenna seemed pretty sure about what she wanted. I do recall that she seemed to be putting some distance between us on this day.

Here is the agreement:

COOPERATIVE AGREEMENT

The following is an informal understanding between Jenna and David and Linda related to the birth, placement, and post-placement relationships between these two parties. This is not set forth as a legally binding agreement; rather it is to be used as an instrument to guide and facilitate continued open communication between the parties involved. It is expected that feelings may change after the baby is born; this agreement should be revised as needed. A willingness of both parties to understand and work with needed changes to this agreement is understood.

The birth parents and adoptive parents accept that the basis of this open-adoption relationship is their trust that each will remain accessible to the other in the years that lie ahead. Any change of names, addresses, phone numbers will be shared with each other and with Providence Place.

1.   Plan for contact from Oct. 6 until labor begins: *We will call each other once per week (Wednesdays after doctor's appointment).*

2.   Plan for contact when labor begins: Jenna will call when she is confirmed in the hospital.

3.   Plan for contact at hospital during labor and delivery: *Ok for David and Linda to be in waiting room at hospital.*

4.   Plan for contact with one another and the baby after delivery and during stay in the hospital: *Ok for David and Linda to spend time in the nursery with the baby. Jenna will decide contact with David and Linda once she is in the hospital.*

5.   Plan for naming the baby: *Jenna is fine with David and Linda's choice of Finley Parker.*

6.   Plan for circumcision if baby boy: *Do it at hospital before discharge.*

7.   Plan for discharge from the hospital: *Jenna and the baby will be discharged separately.*

8.   Plan for signing of the birth parent papers and adoptive parent papers: *Jenna will sign at home.*

9.   Plan for placement ceremony: *No placement ceremony.*

10. Plan for contact after the adoptive family takes baby home: *Jenna will make the first contact. Send pictures every Christmas even if Jenna has not contacted us. Include letter/updates but no video unless Jenna specifically requests.*

11. Plan for subsequent contacts during first six months of placement, plan for expenses to be paid by adoptive parents or birth parents: *David and Linda will continue to pay expenses for six weeks after birth.*

12. Plan for subsequent contacts during the second six months of placement: *See #10.*

13. Specific requests not covered above: *Jenna would like a copy of original birth certificate.*

It is important to remember that this agreement is based on trust, mutual caring, and respect between birth parents and adoptive parents. Open adoption is not shared parenting. Contact between parties will be made with consideration for the privacy of each party and with consent of each party.

It is understood that Providence Place counseling staff remains available to provide mediation or assistance with renegotiation of this agreement.

Signed by: Providence Place Counselor, October 6, 1994

As October wore on with a pending due date of November 8, our emotions ran high. We were excited but nervous and apprehensive, too, since we could not be sure of the outcome. Our counselor reported on her recent meeting with Jenna. She said this time, Jenna seemed happy and talkative. She had lost some fluid in her face and fingers and was more comfortable than during previous visits. In the past, Jenna had often been reserved and had not looked forward to the sessions. But today was different. The counselor gave us a written risk assessment that included the following:

— *At times, Jenna is resistant to confront the depth of her feelings connected with her pregnancy and the adoption plan.*

— Jenna's mother would support a parenting plan.
— Lack of emotional support within her family.
— Although Michael is supportive, the fact that he is not here, but will be here for the birth, could pose a risk.
Recommendation: Proceed with the match with Jenna as planned, taking all risks into consideration and preparing for a variety of outcomes.

When I read this risk report now, I wonder why I was not scared. Jenna's mother supporting a parenting plan was news to us, and we were getting very close to the due date. But at the time, I did not allow myself to think about or prepare for the possibility that Jenna would not place her baby with us. So, no, I was not prepared for a variety of outcomes.

We wanted to see Jenna one more time before the birth, so we asked if we could take her to the butterfly arboretum in Houston. I will never forget that trip. Jenna was so radiant, and her belly was so big. Before we left our house, we both laughed as I sprayed perfume on our shoulders and sleeves in the hope that it would help to attract butterflies. I know Jenna was physically uncomfortable that day, but she wanted to be with us. It was a beautiful sunny day, and it was such a treat walking among the butterflies as they gently landed on our shoulders.

That day Jenna seemed a little distant, and that is when the worry flooded in. *Will she really go through with this? How hard this must be for her.* By the end of the visit, I felt her pulling away, and of course my anxiety was over the top.

Our waiting-couples meeting was in late October at our counselor's home. There were eight couples, and two of us were matched with due dates of November 8th and November 14th. We happily shared our experiences with the other couples. Meeting with other couples going through the same challenges and sharing the same hopes was a blessing and helped us work through our tremendous anxiety.

At the end of October, Jenna phoned to tell us Michael had not returned as planned. They were officially broken up, but he was supposed to arrive that weekend since the baby was due next week. There had been a misunderstanding, and he told her that he never intended on coming until after the baby was born. She was so disappointed because her plan had been for him to be in the delivery room.

But they worked it out, and he agreed to come for the birth. We were relieved for Jenna.

***

With Sofie's adoption, three days after our first meeting with Rachel and Ricky at the mall, the counselor called. The good news was that Rachel had reported that our Sunday meeting was "wonderful." (We thought so too!) Rachel was especially pleased with how we dealt with three-year-old Finley when the toddler fussed. Both she and Ricky were thinking seriously about us, and the meeting had been comfortable. However, they were not ready to match.

One reason was that I worked full time, and we had a nanny; Rachel wanted to think about that. She appreciated that our nanny was the same person every day and especially liked that the caregiver came to our home. But she was still thinking about whether she would prefer a stay-at-home mom. Also, her mother, Kim, who was still in favor of a childless couple, had called two other families. The counselor also shared that she thought Ricky's mother, Beth, was very engaged and described her as bright and sensible.

It took another month, but in July 1998, two months before the birth, we had an official match meeting with Rachel and Ricky. We were elated, but also, we knew we had to prepare ourselves for the journey ahead. During that same meeting, we filled in the cooperative agreement, which reads as follows:

COOPERATIVE AGREEMENT

The following is an informal understanding between David and Linda Sexton and Rachel and Ricky related to the birth, placement, and post-placement relationships between these two parties. This is not set forth as a legally binding agreement; rather, it is to be used as an instrument to guide and facilitate continued open communication between the parties involved. It is expected that feelings may change after the baby is born; this agreement should be revised as needed. A willingness of both parties to understand and work with needed changes to this agreement is understood.

The birth parents and adoptive parents accept that the basis of this open-adoption relationship is their trust that each will remain accessible to the other in the years that lie ahead. Any change of names, addresses, and phone numbers will be shared with each other and with Providence Place.

1.   Plan for contact from July 1998, until labor begins: *Telephone calls between one another. Ricky and Rachel would like to visit in the Sextons' home. Rachel will call after each doctor's appointment.*

2.   Plan for contact when labor begins: *Rachel and Ricky will call the Sextons when labor begins. Ricky will notify Providence Place counselor.*

3.   Plan for contact at hospital during labor and delivery: *Ricky will be Rachel's Lamaze coach. Rachel's mother will be in the delivery room. Sextons will be in the hospital waiting room.*

4.   Plan for contact with one another and the baby after the delivery and during stay in the hospital: *Rachel wants the baby to stay in the room with her. She wants "everyone" to see the baby soon after delivery but also wants privacy with the baby and Ricky.*

5.   Plan for naming the baby: *Girl or boy, Ricky's choice is Raistlin. All parties will discuss between now and delivery.*

6.   Plan for circumcision of baby boy: *Boy will be circumcised.*

7.   Plan for discharge from the hospital, including who gets to keep the hospital mementos, such as baby bracelet, birth certificate, pictures of newborn, etc.: *Will request duplicates of hospital mementos. Newborn pictures will be ordered by Providence Place.*

8.   Plan for signing of the birth parent papers and adoptive parent papers: *Rachel and Ricky think they will want to check out of the hospital and complete paperwork elsewhere. Adoptive parent papers will be signed elsewhere also.*

9.   Plan for entrustment ceremony: *All parties will consider various possibilities and agree on a ceremony. Ricky and Rachel will probably leave first.*

10. Plan for contact after adoptive family takes baby home: *David and Linda will call Rachel and Ricky when they arrive home with the baby.*

11. Plan for subsequent contacts during first six months of placement: *Ricky and Rachel want monthly letters and pictures. Adoptive parents will keep the eight-hundred number for at least six months, and Ricky and Rachel can call at any time. Visits to be discussed.*

12. Plan for subsequent contacts during second six months of placement: *Will be left open for discussion, and visits to be arranged as convenient for all parties.*

13. Specific requests not covered above and plan for all future contact: *Rachel and Ricky want the baby to know he/she is adopted. They want the child to call them by their first names.*

14. Plan for handling "bad news" of whatever kind: *Bad news will be handled by telephone and in person when possible.*

It is important to remember that this agreement is based on trust, mutual caring, and respect between birth parents and adoptive parents. Open adoption is not shared parenting. Contact between parties will be made with the consideration for the privacy of each party and with consent of each party.

It is understood that the Providence Place counseling staff remains available to provide mediation or assistance with renegotiation of this agreement.

Signed by: Providence Place Counselor, Rachel, Ricky, David, and Linda on 7/10/1998

Also, the adoption counselor provided us with an initial risk assessment following the July 10th match and cooperative agreement meeting. Here is her professional risk summary:

— *Rachel and Ricky are young and somewhat immature.*
— *Her family background is possibly dysfunctional. However, her parents are supportive of adoption plans. They do have many concerns about finances but have been reasonable in their requests for assistance.*

— Rachel needs to focus on her own feelings and emotions concerning the baby. Her mother has a definite need to control all situations and may present problems if Rachel does not abide by her wishes.

— Both Rachel and Ricky feel very positive about you and Finley. This should give them peace about their decision if they place the baby.

While this assessment is based on my professional expertise and experience, it is offered with no guarantees or certainties.

Getting closer to the birth date is when things start getting harder for everyone, and it was no easier the second time around. The match dynamics with Rachel and Ricky were very different from our experience with Jenna and Michael. By the time we matched with them in July, Rachel had two months left in her pregnancy. With Jenna, we matched nearly six months before the birth, and we had shared a lot of time with her, so I really got to know her. That was partly because Michael had moved to Alabama, and Jenna lived in the same city as we did, so it was easy to visit. I don't recall ever meeting with only Rachel; it was always her and Ricky and often with other family members too. In retrospect, I did not get to know Rachel in the same way I did Jenna. We met a few times over the next months, but since they lived in Austin and we lived in Houston, the trips needed to be planned well in advance and always included additional family members.

Before Sofie was born, I recall phone conversations with Kim, Rachel's mom. Kim was supportive of the adoption plan and told me about her three girls, Rachel being the youngest. She talked a lot about her challenges, how she was now working for Southwestern Bell and wanted to make it to retirement. As she talked about cooking dinner each night for her family, I could tell she felt stressed and guilty that she could not bring a new baby into her family. She said, "I just can't raise another baby at this point in my life." Talking with Rachel's mom gave me confidence that Rachel had the support she needed to make an adoption plan. I am sure that talking with me helped Kim reconcile the adoption plan too.

Rachel also spoke with me on the phone and had the gift of gab. (Something that Sofie has definitely inherited.) When we were together, Rachel was very talkative. She spoke a lot about her sisters and their relationship with each other. Her oldest sister had already moved out of the house, so she was especially close to her other sister.

Rachel told me that her school wanted to put her in a gifted and talented program, but she did not want that because she didn't like those kids. Her parents agreed she could stay with her friends. I remember thinking, *What parent would not want their child in a gifted and talented program? Why did they give in to her?* Ironically, when Sofie was going into the sixth grade, which was her last year of elementary school, the school asked if they could put her in the gifted and talented class. Sofie was devastated. She was in a class with her group of friends she'd had since first grade, and she wanted to stay with them. Guess what? We gave in to her just like Kim and Rachel's dad had given in to Rachel. Go figure.

I also had phone conversations with Ricky's mom, Beth. She was particularly strong, and I could tell she was holding it together for her family. Though she was honest in telling me that she wanted to raise the baby, she knew Ricky and Rachel did not want that. They had chosen adoption with David and me as the parents. I cannot imagine what Beth and Mark were going through with their teenage boy and his clear ideas. It was important for them to get to know us, too, if this open adoption had a chance of working.

Ricky was the oldest of the four children they were raising. I think Beth decided that if adoption were going to happen with her first grandchild, she would make sure Sofie knew how much her birth father's family loved her. And it was amazing how Beth navigated the relationship with consistency and respect. I learned so much from her over the years.

David and I made another trip to Austin to visit the families before the birth — all arranged by Beth. We went to Ricky's home and met the entire family. The four kids were all on their best behavior. They gave us a tour of their rooms, which they had obviously cleaned for our visit. Ricky wanted to show us the room where he slept, and his little sister, only eight years old, jumped up and down with delight as she showed us her Barbie doll collection. I remember thinking they were such a kind, stable family.

In the dining room, my eye caught a container filled with about twenty tubes of Elmer's glue, which Beth explained she used when she taught Sunday school. I was surprised, thinking, *How do you find the time to raise four children and be a Sunday school teacher?* I did not know Beth then, but I do now, and that was just the tip of the iceberg of what this incredible, strong, and capable woman is made of. Years later, when a friend asked me to teach Sunday school with her, I hesitated. After all, I worked full-time and was raising two children. How could I possibly squeeze that in? But then I thought about Beth, which influenced me to give it a try, and I never looked back. First, I taught Finley's class and later taught Sofie's. Those were many busy but happy and fulfilling years.

About two months before Sofie was born, Rachel and Ricky came to our home in Houston with Ricky's parents, Beth and Mark, for the first time. I made sure that the house was sparkling clean because I wanted to impress them. I set the table with my bright green, purple, and white dishes and matching placemats and napkins. It looked very inviting and festive.

We were all set for their arrival, and I was nervous because we would be talking about baby names. David and I wanted to agree on names with Rachel and Ricky as we thought this was a way to honor them. In addition, we thought it would be nice to be able to tell our child that we named her together.

At the previous cooperative agreement meeting, Ricky had suggested the name Raistlin after a character from a science-fiction series he enjoyed. At this point, we knew Rachel was having a girl, and you can imagine how David and I reacted to naming our baby girl Raistlin! But we did not want to upset them, so we were not too verbal about it. David and I thought we better get into high gear to find alternatives. David suggested Sofia, and it immediately felt warm and right to me, so we agreed to float that name instead.

During lunch, David bravely brought up our name choice. Thankfully, Rachel and Ricky loved it too. What a relief. And I recall Ricky's dad, Mark, liked it as well, since Sofia was a name with a Spanish origin, and Mark was Hispanic. We all agreed that her nickname would be Sofie because we didn't want people to make up other nicknames. That hurdle was crossed.

We then suggested that Rachel and Ricky come up with a middle name for Sofie. Since Finley's middle name was their birth mother's best friend, we wanted Sofie's middle name to directly connect to Rachel and Ricky. They were excited about this and came back a week later with the name Faith. We loved it. So, Sofia Faith was ready to come into this world.

Distractions were a welcome relief for us in the weeks leading up to the birth. About a month before Sofie was born, we had a family beach vacation with my mom and three sisters and their families — all sixteen of us. It is not often that we are all together, so my sisters took this opportunity to put together a surprise baby shower for David, me, and Finley.

We had rented a large beach house to accommodate the entire group and it included a stand-alone garage with a studio apartment on top. We were not using that apartment, so it was a perfect place for my sisters to set up the surprise baby shower. I had just come in from the beach and remember being hot, sweaty, salty, and wet from the ocean when my sisters called us up to the studio apartment. They had transformed it into a party atmosphere complete with cake, decorations, balloons, and gifts. I was touched, but I cried as all the worry and stress surfaced. I did not know if Rachel and Ricky would go through with it, and the celebration brought out my worries and fears. We didn't have any right to celebrate — yet. My family meant well, but it was hard.

PART III – The Births

8. A Heavy Weight

"Come now! They are ready. Hurry!"

— Beth, birth grandmother

The gravity of Finley's upcoming birth and placement was a heavy weight for everyone. Our counselor met with Jenna and Michael together on the due date and called me afterward. She said they had not talked about how this would go, and she could tell they disagreed on some things. Michael said he wanted visits with the baby and us, and Jenna said she did not want visits. This was just the reverse of what they each wanted initially, but if Michael wanted visits, then Jenna did as well. The counselor got the sense that Jenna was still hurting over their breakup.

Then they talked about names on the birth certificate. Michael thought that Jenna wanted her last name on the certificate, and Jenna thought it should be Michael's. She said they needed to talk about this again, but the plan was for Michael to only stay for one and a half weeks.

Jenna had been having some cramps and contractions, and her hospital bag was packed and ready to go. Our counselor expressed that she wished it could work out for these two. I think she sensed a special bond. Ultimately, it did because they were married seventeen years later — it was just a very long road getting there.

The next day Jenna's mom, Susan, called. Jenna had gone to her doctor's appointment that morning and was having pre-labor contractions. Initially, the doctor thought the baby would be born within twenty-four hours and sent Jenna to the hospital. But after an hour or so of monitoring, they sent her home.

Susan shared all the details: Jenna was fifty percent effaced, but her water had not broken yet. The doctor gave her something to help her sleep since she was tired and irritable. Susan canceled her own work for the next three days because the baby would be born soon. She confirmed that Michael was now at his brother's apartment and planned to go to the hospital. Susan also notified our adoption counselor. She told us to stand by and promised to call when there was more news.

It was hard to sleep that night.

There was no news by morning, so David and I went to work as usual. But nothing was usual about that day. David had bought a mobile phone the previous weekend, and I carried it everywhere. In 1994, most people did not have mobile phones, and the reception was not so good. Only Susan had this number, and it was my lifeline to news about Jenna and the baby, so I didn't want to go into a conference room for a meeting because the signal was either too low or nonexistent. I had to be near a window for the phone to work. Unnerving! What if the call could not go through?

Finally, at 2:00 p.m., when I was meeting with two colleagues in my office, the phone rang. I asked them to step out, and it was indeed Susan with the news that Jenna was back in the hospital, and this time they were keeping her. Susan did warn us, however, that it could be a while before the baby was born.

I went into high gear. I called David with the good news, and we agreed to meet shortly. I had been preparing for this moment for weeks, but there was still so much to do. I was not leaving the office for just a day or a week; I planned to be out for three months. I needed to get with my replacement for last-minute updates and decide how to handle those last few emails and phone calls. Back then, you could not just bring your computer home with you.

It all took two hours, and finally, by 4:00 p.m., we were both ready and nervous as we headed to the hospital. But wait! There was one more stressful stop to pick up the extended battery we had ordered for the phone the day before. Then we were off again.

When we arrived at the Women's Atrium at Houston Northwest Medical Center, the woman at the volunteer desk told us that Jenna was in Room 3 in Labor and Delivery. We did not see Susan or Michael since they stayed with Jenna during her long labor. To our surprise, sitting in the waiting room was Michael's father. We had previously talked to him for directions to Michael's high school but had not met him, so we were happy for the opportunity. We were very comfortable with him, and we sensed that he was relieved and pleased once he met us too. At forty years old (and younger than David!), he was a short man who wore glasses and had a mustache. We passed the hours in friendly conversation, learning about each other. He mostly wanted to know how open adoption worked, and we mostly wanted to know about Michael's family history. He was clearly there to support his very young, much-loved son.

He told us Michael was always a sweet kid and loved to explore. One day, as he was driving home from work, he knew right away that Michael had been busy collecting spiders and bugs again when he saw all the water meters without covers. Michael loved insects.

On another day, he came home from work, and a group of kids were gathered around Michael in the driveway. Michael had a water moccasin, a very poisonous snake, in a large jar with his hand over the top and no lid! "Now, that will scare a parent," he said, remembering how he always worried about kids' safety. David shared his own childhood story about skipping across logs on the pond at the paper mill. Very dangerous.

Michael's dad used to work on oil rigs and had often been away from home. He said that was partly why he and Michael's mother ended up in divorce. He now worked in oil field/drilling services and had just returned from New Zealand. His work had also taken him to Argentina, Alaska, and Antarctica. Now, he was remarried and redecorating his home and joked about how hard that was on a marriage.

He told us that Michael had been born at this very same hospital, weighing only five and a half pounds. Michael had been the second twin to come out, and he had looked on in horror when he saw his child, who appeared to have no face.

But soon, the doctor peeled a layer of skin back, and he was fine. The condition is known as being born with a veil, called a caul, which carries a lot of myth. In many cultures, it is a sign of good luck.

After many hours, they sent us home because the baby had still not arrived. Poor Jenna was still in labor.

We went back to the hospital the following morning, and still no baby. Then at 11:14 a.m. on that November day in 1994, after more than thirty hours of labor, Finley was born. But we could not yet see the baby. There were complications because the umbilical cord had been wrapped around the baby's neck, causing Finley to suffer some lack of oxygen, so they went directly into the Neonatal Intensive Care Unit (NICU).

Jenna and Michael did not ask to see us either. Jenna's sister and father were at the hospital by then, and we met them briefly for the first time. They, of course, had seen Jenna and the baby, but we had not been invited in, which left us feeling isolated and a little hurt. Still, we fully understood Jenna's need for privacy.

We waited and waited, but the hospital could not let us see the baby in the NICU since Jenna had not signed any papers giving us permission. One of the nurses was sympathetic to our plight and said she would try to get the NICU doctor to call us but could not promise anything. Of course, we were worried sick, not knowing the baby's condition.

After many hours, we went to dinner near the hospital. To our surprise, the cell phone rang — a call from the NICU doctor. Finley was doing well but would need to stay in the hospital for a few more days. However, he said the baby would be fine, which calmed our fears.

We could do nothing but go home that night.

By the next day, Jenna had given the hospital permission for us to see Finley. We went into the NICU and saw this beautiful little baby with an IV coming right out of the top of their head. The nurse let me sit and hold Finley, and it was tricky with all the wires and tubes, but it was the happiest moment ever.

Jenna and Michael joined us in the NICU. She and Michael both held Finley, and I was able to take some pictures. It was so emotional, and Jenna looked very tired. I couldn't even begin to imagine her pain, and I understood why she was not looking forward to seeing us.

Jenna was released from the hospital soon after, but Finley was not. We stayed and held the baby for hours. The nurses were so kind. One told us her sister had a baby as a teenager and made an adoption plan, and the nurse had always questioned that decision. She said watching us with Finley made her understand for the first time just how much adoptive couples want to be parents. She realized that adoption may have been a good choice for her sister.

The following hours were tough. Our counselor was with Jenna at her home and reported that Jenna was having difficulty signing the papers. What mixed emotions. We loved Jenna, and we felt deeply for her pain. At the same time, we prayed that she would have the strength to sign. Then we prayed that whatever the outcome, we would graciously accept it. Adoption is complex and there are so many opposite emotions going on at the same time. We did not want Jenna to hurt and at the same time we really wanted a baby. So many competing emotions co-existed.

We were at the hospital with baby Finley when the call we had been waiting for came that evening. Jenna had signed, and our counselor needed to meet us to get Finley released. Surprise. Relief.

It was already dark. David had gone into work but left early to come to the hospital to see Finley, not knowing when, or if, we would bring the baby home. I think we came in two cars because we were afraid to plan on it. It was just easier not to set our expectations that day.

We had the car seat ready to go in my Infiniti G20, and David had his Mazda. By the time all the paperwork was done, I was too nervous to drive the baby home. I don't know why, but I was, so David agreed to drive my car, and I drove his. It was a forty-five-minute drive on the freeway at night, so our cars could not easily stay together on the road.

David said later that he could not hear Finley in the back seat as he drove. The baby was so quiet that he was afraid that he may have strapped the seat too tight. *What if the baby could not breathe?* He ended up pulling over in the freeway breakdown lane to check. Finley was fine, but it took him ten minutes to re-enter the freeway with the heavy traffic buzzing by. We both made it home, and so our new life began.

***

The second time around was no easier, but that time we knew our role was to be available, just in case Rachel and Ricky wanted to see us.

I got the call from Rachel's mom, Kim, that Rachel had gone into labor. Finley was just shy of four years old, and my mom had come to Texas from Pittsburgh to take care of Finley, so we were ready. We drove to Austin, straight to the hospital. I remember sitting for hours in an empty waiting room — just David and me. The other family members must have been in a different room. Rachel's sister joined us at some point for a little while, and we were grateful for that.

Just as with our previous experience with Finley's birth parents, the way Rachel and Ricky handled the hours and days after Sofie's birth was not what we had imagined.

When Sofie was born that afternoon in September 1998 at 4:37 p.m., Ricky's mom, Beth, came to tell us the news. She then led us into the birthing room for just a minute to see Sofie, Rachel, and Ricky. It was amazing to see little Sofie. She was perfect, but the mood was solemn. They were not happy to see us at that moment, and we were whisked out. Who could blame them?

The next day, we went to the hospital hoping to see Sofie, but it was not meant to be. We were comforted by our interactions with the birth grandmothers that day. We sat with Kim, Rachel's mom, for some time outside the hospital while we waited. Since she was a smoker and we were all nervous, sitting outside helped. Kim was gracious as she expressed her gratitude for our being there and for the adoption plan. Beth, Ricky's mom, also recalls asking the pediatrician to speak with us about Sofie's health and assure us that she was a healthy baby. We were so fortunate to have these birth-grandmother relationships, and we knew that they, too, were dealing with profound loss and grief.

David and I were alone and isolated while we waited, hoping to get a chance to hold the baby. But that would have to wait.

Since all of Ricky's family was at the hospital visiting Sofie, Beth was kind enough to invite us to lunch with them. Ricky, of course, stayed in the hospital with Rachel and Sofie. At a nearby Mexican restaurant, we joined Beth, Ricky's dad, Mark, and their three other children, along with Mark's parents, Clara and Zeke, who we were meeting for the first time. Beth recently reminded me that during that lunch, Zeke announced, not unkindly, "We don't give away our kids." He was trying to tell us that adoption is not usually an option in Hispanic culture. I know his son Mark, Sofie's birth grandfather, felt that deeply, too. He was still trying to process the adoption decision.

After that day, Sofie's birth great-grandparents Clara and Zeke never missed one of Sofie's birthdays and sent her a card with a two-dollar bill each year. They always called Sofie on her birthday, and we would have a lovely conversation. When Sofie was twenty-two years old, she and I traveled to San Antonio and made our way to see her birth great-grandmother Clara, along with Ricky's aunts and uncles. Sofie was Clara's first great-grandchild, and even though she subsequently had many more, it is clear that not a day goes by that Sofie is not in her thoughts and especially her prayers.

Ricky and Rachel stayed together in the hospital room with Sofie for two nights, and we did not see them. With Finley, we were able to visit the NICU and hold the baby. But Sofie was in the room with Rachel and Ricky, and only their families and friends were allowed in. In retrospect, I believe that those two days and nights with Sofie close to Rachel and Ricky helped her a great deal. She gently came into this world and was not pulled from her familiar birth mother. I am no expert, but I believe this contributed to Sofie being a much calmer, more contented baby and perhaps not feeling abandoned in the same intense way that Finley may have felt. Because Finley needed to be in the NICU, Jenna never got the chance to gently transition them into this world. Jenna held Finley, of course, but mostly the baby was in the NICU. It was an abrupt entrance, and I believe that little baby suffered from grief and loss of the mother bond from the very beginning.

We went back to our hotel room, knowing there was nothing we could do but wait. In the four years since Finley's birth, the law had changed from a twenty-four-hour to a forty-eight-hour waiting period after the birth, before a mother could relinquish her parental rights. My personal feeling is that this was a good change in the law. And Ricky, unlike Michael, had not relinquished his parental rights ahead of time so he too needed to sign papers.

David and I went to see a movie that night — *Saving Private Ryan* — just to keep our minds busy. I cried throughout it. Not a good choice.

The next day, when the forty-eight hours were almost up, David and I went to a nearby restaurant — just waiting and praying. We were not expecting a call since we knew they needed more time. Suddenly Beth called me and said, "Come now! They are ready. Hurry!"

We met at the hospital chapel at 7:00 p.m. Everyone was there: Rachel and her parents and sister, along with Ricky and his parents and siblings. Rachel's sister recited an entrustment prayer. It read in part:

"We are all adopted children in God's sight. Ephesians chapter 1, verses four and five, tells us God chose us in him before the world began, to be holy and blameless in his sight. To be full of love; he likewise predestined us through Jesus Christ to be his adopted sons and daughters — such was his will... We do not always understand God's plan for our lives, but we know he loves us, and he will keep us in the palm of his hand. Let us pray for those who are a part of God's plan for Sofia."

We listened to the prayer, but honestly, it did not help ease the pain for anyone.

Rachel and Ricky chose to have an entrustment ceremony in the chapel that day. To face the reality of what placing your child for adoption really means in such a symbolic and meaningful way was a brave thing to do.

Rachel handed Sofie to me, and I stood there holding her as each person kissed her. They gave us items that were precious to them: a rosary, a St. Christopher medal, Ricky's treasured cross from his Catholic confirmation, and a family picture from 1984. There wasn't a dry eye in the chapel.

Then they all left, and David and I were standing there alone, holding Sofie. It was the most tender moment I have ever experienced in my entire life. We probably needed to sign some paperwork with the counselor that night, but I cannot remember doing that. I was overwhelmed with gratitude and deep sadness for Rachel and Ricky and their families. Our joy would have to wait a little longer.

We looked at each other and decided we had better get her in the car and get home to Houston. We made the two-and-a-half-hour trip as carefully as we could. David drove, and I sat in the back seat beside Sofie's carrier, and she stayed fast asleep the whole time. When we arrived home, I was so grateful that my mother and Finley were there to greet us. I think that night was the first time in two days that I slept. A few days later, David's mom came, too, and it was magical having both grandmothers doting on our two precious children at the same time.

It did not take long for our joy to come pouring in. We were thrilled beyond all measure to welcome this beautiful baby into our home. And we were so grateful to Rachel and Ricky for entrusting us to be Sofie's parents. Finley loved being a big sibling. David adored both children and fussed at getting the car seats just right. I loved the bath-time play and the sweet smell of my clean babies. The joy of dressing them alike in beautiful clothes, singing songs, and reading bedtime books was such a gift that I never took for granted.

9. First Forty-Eight Hours

"I knew that adoption was the right thing for Sofie. I was not changing my mind; I just wanted her to myself for those two days in the hospital."

— Rachel, birth mother

I asked Jenna and Michael what they remember about those first twenty-four to forty-eight hours at the hospital, imagining that they were some of the most difficult hours of their lives.

Jenna said, "I would not say that was the hardest; there were a lot of hard things in my life. That moment for me was weird because I had never experienced anything like it and had no context." She explained that trauma does not engrain itself in your memory. Her memory of it is dissociative — there are only bits and pieces — vignettes. She recalls after the birth being in the hospital, completely dazed and confused, not even knowing where she was, and in absolute despair.

A nurse found her wandering around and brought her back to her room. She remembers feeling anticipation for the moment of birth, and then after it happened, she felt so empty. There was a lot of grief. She had gotten so used to Finley being in her womb, during which she would talk and sing to her baby. Finley was the closest person she had, and then the baby was gone. She felt so alone.

Although she and Michael had broken up over the phone the previous month, he had come back from Alabama for the birth. I can just imagine that their reunion right before Finley was born was not much of a comfort to Jenna. Michael even talked about the birth later and said that while he tried to comfort Jenna during the delivery, he was unable. He said the only thing that gave her comfort was the epidural. Clearly, the birth experience was hard for both of them.

***

I asked Rachel about those first forty-eight hours after the birth. What was it like for her? She was amazed at how immediately her protective instincts kicked in. Knowing that she only had two days with Sofie, she did not want nurses and other people to talk to her or care for the baby. She wanted to be alone in the room with Sofie and Ricky, to soak up those two days. "It was hard," she said, "because in the hospital, there was always someone coming in to take the baby or change her diaper." Wanting to be the only one to care for Sofie, she told them, "No, no, I am doing that."

Rachel never wavered on her choice to make an adoption plan, but Ricky did a bit. She recalls him saying, "Maybe we shouldn't do this. Maybe I can get a job." They cried together and wished things were different.

Rachel knew what she would do the entire time; she just wanted to pretend for two days. She breastfed Sofie because she wanted the experience, though she kept it a secret — afraid everybody would freak if she bonded with the baby too much and could not go through with the adoption.

Dealing with her feelings when visitors came in was not easy. Some of their friends came to see Sofie, but Rachel did not want them there for long. When Ricky's entire family arrived, she had to work hard to tell herself it was their time with the baby too. The hormones were powerful, and she had to make herself sit on the other bed to give them time with Sofie because she was feeling way too protective. She did not want to be too selfish. Looking back, she does not know how she was able to compartmentalize her feelings. It all went by really fast.

Rachel also said that when the Providence Place counselor came, she did not want her there. She told her that she was not changing her mind; she just wanted alone time.

Then it was time to go to the chapel for the entrustment ceremony. It was a painful moment but also one of affirmation for Rachel. When she walked into the chapel and saw David and me, she could tell by our faces that we were feeling her pain. She was so grateful for that moment. Seeing the emotion on our faces helped her go through with it. She said, "It gave me comfort that I made the right choice for Sofie and for me." She just had to trust herself, accept that she was doing the right thing, and not let her instincts take over. She even told me that she was so grateful that we were sad but that she felt guilty about it. Because when she saw us in the chapel, she had the exact same feeling as the first time she met us — a feeling that reaffirmed we were the right parents for Sofie. Though she had had several affirmations after meeting us, this was the final one. "These are definitely the right people."

To this day, I recall the overwhelming feeling of sadness and emotion in the chapel that evening. Even after everyone left, and I was holding that precious baby in my arms, I could not feel joy, not yet.

***

I asked Ricky about those first forty-eight hours after the birth. His memory comes in bits and pieces too. He remembers being extremely emotional, and when he was asked to cut the umbilical cord, he just couldn't do it. The doctor and nurses had talked about how young he and Rachel were. Rachel's mom shouted for joy when Sofie was born. He remembers lying on the hospital bed and seeing Sofie in the little crib and Rachel trying to breastfeed her.

And he recalls being exasperated at the Providence Place counselor because they kept coming in telling them repeatedly what would happen and how things would work.

He remembers holding Rachel because she was distraught. There was a lot of second-guessing. "Did we do the right thing?" He tried hard to keep Rachel's spirits up by talking about how they would visit Sofie and us.

I asked Ricky what he remembers about the entrustment ceremony in the chapel. He asked, "What ceremony?" He did not remember it. I can relate because when I have gone through a traumatic emotional experience, like when I was seven and my parents divorced and my dad left, my coping mechanism was to forget. The entrustment ceremony was probably so traumatic that Ricky blocked it out. He erased the event from his memory.

But he could not erase the real pain that came after they left the hospital. He spent that first week back in his old habits, just trying to drown those emotions.

Rachel told me that she always admired how Ricky could express his feelings. He talked about them, he cried about them, he wrote about them. Rachel had a much more difficult time expressing herself — especially to us. So, Ricky often took the lead. He wrote this beautiful handwritten note to Sofie on the day she was born. It is included here with permission from Ricky and Sofie:

To my dearest, most precious gift of love,

My love, I write this letter to express my feelings and actions on this day of your birth. Let me start by saying how much your mother and I love you. So much, in fact, that Rachel and I are making the hardest decision of our lives to give you the life you so greatly deserve. We are placing you in the love and care of David and Linda Sexton, the two greatest people in this world, besides you and your mother. Your mother and I are giving up our responsibility as your caretakers so that you can have everything in life that we cannot offer. As I look into your darling face, I feel a love and passion for something that I have never felt before. And as I look to the future and what I must do, I feel a pain unparalleled to any I've ever encountered. To give up my own daughter, my flesh and blood, my heart and soul, my everything, I'd rather die. But as I watch you so beautifully sleeping, so perfect and immaculate in every way, I realize what I must do.

My dearest Sofia, for nine months, I have watched you grow inside your mother, and for nine months, I have been anticipating this day. I kiss and hold you as your father, even to know that you are only mine for forty-eight tiny hours. But after watching and praying over your beautiful visage, I know that I am doing the right thing. And my greatest hope is that someday when you are older, you will understand this. What we are doing is out of our undying love for you and no other reason. Your mother and I love you with all our hearts, and if you ever need anything, I will lay down my life to provide it. I love you, Sofia!

Love always and forever,

Your Father,

Ricky

(P.S. You are the best thing that ever happened to me, and I thank God every day for you.)

PART IV– Parenting Journey Begins

10. Change of Plan

"Because you may be experiencing emotions that you didn't ex-pect…or were unprepared for, you may be unsure of how to interact with each other. You need to be honest with yourself and with each other."

— The Open Adoption Experience, *Melina and Roszia*

After Finley was born, things changed for Jenna but not for Michael. Jenna wanted more visitation, which we were happy about, and Michael stuck to his original plan.

I thought it would be pure joy bringing Finley home from the hospital. But at first, it wasn't. No one can truly anticipate how the birth parents and adoptive parents will feel after the birth. I could not stop thinking about Jenna. It was unfair that our joy and gratitude were so immense, while Jenna was torn between grief and gratitude. It felt empty that we could not just pick up the phone and talk to her since our agreement was that she would make the first contact. She needed some time.

But it did not take too long for Jenna to call. She felt very differently after Finley was born. Instead of wanting only pictures and letters as she had first re-quested, she wanted visitation. Now she wanted to visit Finley, and she wanted to change the terms of our co-op agreement. We set a date to meet Jenna and Susan at a restaurant near them. We were looking forward to seeing Jenna and, at the same time, nervous about how she would react to seeing the baby.

With much anticipation, excitement, fear, and love, David and I put one-month-old Finley in the car and drove to meet Jenna and Susan at Uncle Tom's Kitchen restaurant in Spring, Texas. They wanted so much to see and hold the baby. We were late due to traffic, so the drive took nearly one and a half hours. When we finally arrived, Jenna and Susan were sitting in the front of the restaurant sipping iced tea as they waited. In those days, there was no cell phone texting, so I can only imagine how hard that wait was for them.

After switching to a nonsmoking section in the back for some privacy, we placed Finley, still in the car carrier, on the table. Before we even sat down, Susan gathered the baby in her arms for a hug and to say hello. Finley was much too young to respond but must have felt the love. Jenna smiled as Susan handed Finley to her. Jenna was a little awkward and anxious, and then baby Finley began to fuss. All of us tried to settle the baby down. Luckily, there was a mirror behind our booth that caught the baby's eye. Susan was able to hold Finley over her shoulder, and Finley was amused for a little while. When dinner arrived, all four of us took turns holding the baby, so we could eat.

I was so touched that Susan brought a special gift for Finley — Jenna's baby blanket. Susan had embroidered *Jenna D.C. (Jenna's last name and birth date)—1:29 A.M.* on it when Jenna was born, and underneath it, she had embroidered *Finley P.C. (Jenna's last name and Finley's birth date)—11:14 A.M.* The day Finley was born, the baby carried Jenna's last name, and the day of the adoption decree six months later, our child became a Sexton. This baby blanket was the most treasured gift imaginable.

When the baby needed a diaper change, I got up to go to the restroom and asked Jenna if she wanted to come with me. She did. I changed Finley and then Jenna gently cradled and carried the baby back to our table with so much care.

Then came our moment of truth. What would Jenna's request be? I was pretty sure that Susan had a lot to do with Jenna's confidence in wanting to have further contact and visitation with us. As a mother to a grieving child, it made sense that Susan would encourage Jenna to see the baby. Jenna tried hard to protect everyone in her life, and I think, sometimes, she played the role of mother to Susan, so it was nice seeing the support Jenna had from her mom this night. We agreed that we would discuss contact for the next six months, so it was comfortable for everyone not to make any lifelong decisions just then.

When we asked Jenna what she wanted for contact, she said she wanted to see us every three weeks. Wow! We did not expect that. David and I had agreed that three visits over the next six months would be nice, so a request for every three weeks surprised us. But we talked and quickly came to a loving solution, agreeing to calendar three visits. The first would be Finley's baptism on January 8th; the second would be February 25th on a Saturday, so Jenna could come with her friend Parker; and the third would be April 15th, Easter weekend, another Saturday, so Jenna could come with her sister. We also agreed that Jenna could call us any time she wanted to visit. If we had plans, she would understand, but if we didn't, she was always welcome.

Jenna then explained with tears in her eyes that our friendship had meant a lot to her. She went on to say that she saw me as a big sister and valued her relationship with David too. It was not just the baby she wanted to visit; she wanted to see us. Few things in life have touched me so deeply. This beautiful, brave young woman was the mother of my child, and she cared very much about the baby and me. I began to understand how much we each cherished our bond. I grew to love Jenna, so I was genuinely happy that she wanted to visit. I did not want to let go of her.

Soon after that David, Jenna, and I took baby Finley to the Providence Place waiting-couples meetings once or twice. We presented our story together to demonstrate that open adoption is a good, healthy option, and that it can work. Jenna learned a lot in doing that, namely that volunteer work bolstered her confidence, and educating people and talking about teen pregnancy helped her identify who she was. She also discovered that she was good at standing up in front of people and presenting. She had a knack for it. Plugging in and being part of something bigger than herself helped. The agency was part of that. (Today, she often conducts training sessions on mental health issues and credits this early experience, in part, for her growth.)

***

I was more prepared to remain flexible the second time around, so when Rachel called just a few days after we brought Sofie home, we were happy to make plans to see her that very same week.

Friends and family often asked if I was afraid or felt threatened that Jenna or Rachel would change her mind and want the baby back, especially after visiting with us. That fear that I had early on, surfaced only occasionally after the baby was placed with us. For me, the visits helped ease any lingering worry. They helped both of us grow our love and appreciation for each other.

11. Monthly Reports

"Visiting with Finley was my joy. It was the one thing I was proud of. It was proof that I was a good person."

— Jenna, birth mother

Over the first six months, we were required to write monthly reports to the adoption agency about how Finley was doing and how our family was adjusting. The themes throughout these letters were about Finley's health, growth, and firsts. It was fun to record these milestones. I recall doing this with pride but also with some resentment. What if every parent were required to send some authority monthly photos and updates on their baby's progress? It was a lot of work on top of a full-time job and taking care of an infant. However, I was happy to move one step closer to that adoption date. It was also suggested that we include any interactions with the birth family in the monthly reports. I will share the excerpts from my letters that include comments about my interactions with Jenna.

December 12, 1994 — excerpt from the first-month report:

"We have talked with Jenna several times in the last month. At her request, we met to rework the cooperative agreement. We are having to adjust to Jenna's needs, but everything is working very well. Our visit with her and her mom and Finley last Wednesday was very enjoyable for all of us. Our new agreement states the following: Jenna can call anytime. Linda will send pictures and updates as I have them — about once every month. We have three scheduled visits: January 8th for the baptism, February 25th with Jenna and her friend, April 15th with Jenna and her sister."

When Finley was five weeks old, Jenna called and asked if she could visit and bring Parker and Parker's boyfriend. Parker had not been to our place, and Jenna wanted to show off Finley's new home. We had a great visit and an enjoyable time drinking coffee, eating Christmas cookies, hugging Finley, and taking pictures. Finley was an angel.

Since it was Parker's birthday, I wanted to get her and Jenna something special. I found two beautiful porcelain baby angels at a local gift shop, each wearing a crown of green leaves and holding a candle. I gave one to each girl. I also gave Jenna a guardian angel pin and card, and with smiles, gratitude, and tears, we hugged each other.

Before I knew it, they were back to being teenagers. They left for Astro World, the large Houston amusement park, to ride roller coasters and have some birthday fun. We were worried that it was too cold, so we gave Jenna David's jacket to stay warm.

Later that day, some of our friends came by to see the baby and give us a gift. By the end of the day, I was exhausted and emotionally drained, but very happy.

January 5, 1995 — excerpt from the second-month report:

"Coming up also is Finley's baptism. The baby will be baptized at St. Stephen's Episcopal Church here in Houston on Sunday, January 8th. Jenna and Jenna's mother, Susan, will attend (we hope). It will be a very special occasion for all of us."

Also, in this report, I asked for (and was granted) permission to fly Finley with us to Pittsburgh to visit my mother and sister, who had just had a baby on January 4th. We were thrilled that Finley would have a cousin their age. Our legal papers did not allow us to take the child out of Texas without agency permission.

Finley was baptized at St. Stephens Episcopal Church, Sunday at 9:00 a.m. as planned. Jenna, thankfully, was able to make it. I know it was hard for her to arrange the trip, but she was determined. The day before, she called to tell us that her mom could not make it and asked if we minded if she came with Parker instead. Of course, we said that would be fine. She told us that her mom had been sick and had missed so much work that it was not good for her to miss that Sunday too.

Then our phone rang early Sunday morning with a call from Jenna. Parker could not make it either, but she had a friend who could drive her and her sister to the church. She wanted to know if we could give her and her sister a ride after our planned brunch since the friend could not stay. Yes, of course, we were happy to do that.

We arrived at the church early with Finley's godparents and went to the area where the regulars gathered. We showed off baby Finley, took a few photos, then went to the front of the church, constantly looking back to see if Jenna had arrived. Minutes before 9:00 a.m., we spotted Jenna, her sister, and friend in the back of the church and waved them up to join us in front. The service and ceremony were beautiful. God was with us that day, and I was grateful that Jenna was there. It felt so right.

After the ceremony, we went back to our house for brunch and took lots of pictures in the back yard because the weather was perfect for a January day in Texas. Too soon, it was time to go. Our friends who lived near Jenna were also there and offered to drive her home. This worked out since her sister needed a ride in the opposite direction to the Greyhound bus station downtown, and David and I could take her there. It was the end of Christmas break, and, sadly, her sister needed to return to her father's home in Corpus Christi. Jenna cried as they parted.

That January, I turned thirty-eight, and it was one of the happiest birthdays of my life. I was at home with Finley and loved taking care of the baby. During those days, a highlight was getting together with my friend who had also just adopted a baby. We went to lunch or shopped together and proudly showed off our bundles of joy to anyone who wanted to fuss over them.

I had worked full-time for the past fifteen years, and taking three months off for personal leave was such a joy. At that time, there was no such thing as parental leave for an adoption, so I had to take personal leave without pay. Fortunately, most companies today treat an adoption leave as parental leave and will provide some compensation for the new parents.

After searching for a nanny for several weeks, I hired one. I screened forty-five candidates, conducted eight interviews, and finally found the perfect nanny. Her references were outstanding, and she had the sweetest disposition, along with eleven years of experience. David and I loved her. More importantly, Finley was comfortable with her too. Our instincts about this nanny turned out to be spot-on. Even now, twenty-eight years later, we keep in touch with her.

That same month, I learned something about Jenna from someone who knew her well. He told me that Jenna was thinking about not visiting anymore. He said the visits were hard for her, and they hurt too much. She was having difficulty thinking about this because she felt so much love when she came to our home, and it was hard for her to give that up. I think it was after her visits that the pain came. I thought maybe I would call her, but the phone at Susan's place had been disconnected. So, I wrote Jenna a letter and sent some pictures instead. Thankfully, she did continue to visit us, but I was grateful to know just how hard it was for her. Our visits were always so enjoyable that one could be fooled into thinking that Jenna was doing just fine.

February 1, 1995 — third-month report:

Covered the baptism visit with Jenna and her sister.

March 4, 1995 — excerpt from fourth-month report:

"Last weekend, Jenna came to visit. It was very nice seeing her. She seems to be doing ok, although staying in school is a bit of a challenge because of numerous challenges with her mother and her home life. Finley is really a joy for her, and she is so proud of the baby. We know these visits are good for Jenna, and we plan to see her again in April."

April 9, 1995 — excerpt from fifth-month report:

"We are planning to visit with Jenna and her sister next Saturday. We have only heard from Jenna once in the last several weeks, and she sounded pretty good. She told me that she found a birth-mother support group, and that has helped her a great deal. She did mention that she wished that she could have been part of a birth-mother support group through Providence Place. I mention this in case you are considering groups for birth mothers in areas outside of San Antonio.

Jenna has moved and is now without a phone, so we cannot reach her easily. I continue to send her notes/cards via her girlfriend's address. This seems to be working out fine."

That May, the night before our adoption court date, we arrived in San Antonio with Finley and decided to go out for a special dinner at Morton's Steakhouse. The baby was especially calm and happy that night. We must have had a special glow as we arrived at the restaurant with Finley because the staff asked us what we were celebrating. When we shared that we were there to finalize our adoption, they went out of their way to take care of us. Even the chef came to our table to wish us well, and the entire staff saw us off as we departed. It was a joyful evening, and we will always carry that happy memory with us.

Our Adoption Court Day finally arrived. In Texas, the formal adoption happens at least six months after the placement and only after the agency recommends to the courts that the adoption should go through. We showed up at court, accompanied by Finley's godparents and David's mom. David was all dressed up in a suit and tie but wearing sneakers! Why sneakers? It just did not look right with the outfit. He said he wanted to be ready to take Finley and run if any strangers showed up to claim the baby. *What?* Where had this fear come from? A full legal background review had been done, and the hurdles with potential Native American background had been cleared. Nevertheless, David had been worried that a stranger representing a tribe could arrive and make a claim to the baby.

I laughed about it then, but now I realize how stressful it was for both of us, especially David, until those final papers were signed. And even once they were signed, we thought about loopholes — what if Jenna came back and told the judge she'd changed her mind? Could the judge reverse the adoption? Or what if Michael said he wasn't thinking straight when he signed — could it be reversed? Unreasonable fears, perhaps, but this is what went through our minds.

May 21, 1995 — excerpt from the sixth and final-month report:

"We are also looking forward to taking Finley to a waiting-couples meeting in a few weeks. It looks like Jenna will come with us too. We are very pleased about that. We remember as a waiting couple, the most memorable and helpful meetings were the few where we were able to listen to an adoptive couple along with their birth mother. I think Jenna is looking forward to the meeting too."

Jenna accompanied the three of us to the meeting and was open and transparent. She was brave, and I was proud of her as we told our story with smiles. Recently, as Jenna and I discussed this, she felt that perhaps our symbol of a happy family sitting next to her with all smiles did not even begin to convey the story's fullness, and we never commented on the grief and loss. Neither of us knew much about dealing with both the birth mother and the child's loss. We agreed that post-placement counseling and training for all of us would have been appropriate in those early days.

That May, I received the greatest gift from Jenna — a Mother's Day card. I did not expect this, and it touched me deeply. I'm sure I cried. For Jenna to acknowledge me in this way was beyond anything I had ever imagined.

Even though they were no longer a couple, Michael and Jenna visited together when Finley was about three years old. We were happy to see Michael because we had not seen him since the hospital visit when Finley was two days old. He had joined the military, and although we exchanged cards and photos through the mail, we did not see him again after this visit until Finley was seventeen years old.

We put Finley in a preschool program for early development. We found a great school, and our friend group quickly became other couples with children the same age. It was a fun time experiencing everything from the Houston rodeo to the zoo and the children's museum with our little one. We could not have been happier.

Finley's personality was beginning to emerge too. On one visit to the Houston Zoo, we had the opportunity to let Finley play in the splash fountains that were set up outside in the park for the little ones. It was a hot day and Finley squealed with delight running through the fountains and chasing the next one to pop up. In a flash, Finley removed every stitch of clothing and ran naked from fountain to fountain. Of course, catching Finley without getting soaked ourselves was impossible. When I look back, I realize now that the ability to live and enjoy the moment is a great personality trait, even though I did not appreciate it that day!

Having Jenna in our lives was part of our happiness too. I remember her pulling up one day in a truck, wearing a baseball cap and a big smile. Although she was always happy to see and play with Finley, she was not very physical with the toddler and rarely held or hugged the child for too long. I think that was just Jenna's nature, but maybe, too, holding Finley and close physical contact was hard emotionally, and she may have been protecting herself. I didn't realize just how hard these visits were on Jenna since her smile and face glowed with delight the moment she stepped into our home.

One memorable visit was when Jenna came to our home with her fiancé. The visit was as much about getting to know them as a couple as it was about seeing Finley. This was about the time we had that conversation about what Finley should call Jenna. We all agreed that it would be comfortable for Finley to just call Jenna by her first name. For us it was a simple and uncomplicated solution. Somehow what I remember most about that visit was that Jenna's fiancé had just taken a job as a manufacturer's rep to sell water filtration systems. He took our entire kitchen faucet apart and taught us all about the problems with our water source.

Then Jenna and her fiancé moved to Dallas, and we did not see her for many months. One day, she called to ask if Finley could be a flower child in her wedding — they had set a wedding date. We were thrilled but worried if it was the right thing for Finley. After some thought, we said yes, secretly proud of ourselves for being so mature and open. We did, however, have one remaining concern. Because it had been a while since our last visit, we thought Finley might have difficulty being in the wedding party and walking down the aisle. We asked Jenna and her fiancé if they could visit before the wedding, and to our delight, they were happy to.

Finley was four and a half years old when Jenna married. The formal wedding was beautiful, and we met many of Jenna's relatives. We sat near the front of the church so that Finley could see us. As the wedding party stood near the altar during the ceremony, facing the church pews, Finley spotted us. I could see that they were scared. When I smiled, Finley broke away from the wedding party, ran down the stage steps, and came to sit on my lap. In my heart, I was proud that my child had run to me. I also remember the feeling that people at the wedding were watching us. But I didn't mind. I took many pictures that day and then made two identical photo books — one for Jenna and one for Finley.

***

Ricky and Rachel both left their regular high school after Sofie was born and went to an alternative high school to finish together. I think they got some support there, but most importantly, they had each other and their families.

On the surface, it seemed that Rachel and Ricky were doing well — they were at least going through the motions.

Just like when we adopted Finley, we were required to write monthly reports about how Sofia was doing and how our family was adjusting over our first six months with her. These reports also included photos as well as pediatrician reports. A theme throughout these letters was how healthy, sweet, content, and calm baby Sofia was and how well Finley was adjusting to their new sibling. Again, I will share the verbatim excerpts from my letters that discuss our birth family interactions.

October 8, 1998 — excerpt from the first-month report:

*"We are also happy to report that both Rachel and Ricky seem to be doing well.
Rachel and her father came to visit when Sofia was one week old. They drove to
Houston from Austin and spent three to four hours with us. It was a very nice
visit. My mom was still in town for her month-long visit, and I was grateful to
be able to introduce them to each other. They liked each other very much. Sofia
slept most of the time but did wake up, and Rachel was able to feed her and
hold her for a while. We think it was a good visit for all of us. Rachel was able
to express both her sadness as well as confirm to us that she believed she made
the very best decision for Sofia. It helped to reassure us, and we think the visit
did the same for her. Since that time, we talked on the phone about once a week.
She sounds anxious to get back to school, although she is waiting for her six-week
postpartum checkup before she goes back. Also, Ricky and Rachel each called us
last week to tell us that they have broken up. They seem to be having a difficult
time right now with the breakup, but each expressed a need to date other people
due to their young ages. We really hope it works out well for both of them.*

*Ricky had scheduled a couple of visits with us (September 20th and October 4th)
but had to cancel each of them due to various reasons. We are now rescheduled
to see him and his father, Mark, on October 18th. We have spoken with Ricky
several times over the past weeks, and he seems to be doing fine. He is back at
school and still working at a dry cleaners. He tells us that he likes his new school
very much. We have also spoken with his mother, Beth, who was very supportive
during the entire process, and she reports all is well with her family.*

*We have also spoken to Kim, Rachel's mom, a few times over the past three
weeks, and she expressed her thanks. She and her family sent us a very nice card,
thanking us for the hospital experience and our consideration of Rachel's feelings
during this difficult time. It really touched us to receive this card.*

*We feel like things have settled down quite a bit with both birth families and
are really reassured about the entire open adoption process. We have two more
visits scheduled with Rachel and Ricky in November, on Rachel's sixteenth*

birthday, and in January. At this point, they plan to make them together, even with the breakup, but we will remain flexible as we know plans can always change."

Reading these notes from the first month, I am most struck that Rachel's dad drove her three hours to see Sofie only one week after she was born. I could only imagine the depth of her sadness, but in my heart, I thought that it was good for Rachel to witness our joy and gratitude, hoping that this was all part of the healing process for her.

November 6, 1998 — excerpt from second-month report:

"We also spoke this week with Ricky, Rachel, and Kim (Rachel's mom). They all seem to be doing fine and are looking forward to their visit in November. We think all three of them will come and spend the afternoon. Rachel sounds good on the phone. She has a new job as a cashier at a dry cleaners and seems to really be enjoying the independence that a paycheck of her own brings. She talks of going back to school in a few weeks, and we really hope this works out.

Ricky seems to be doing well in his new school. He and Rachel are back together, and Ricky is especially thrilled to still be seeing Rachel. We also hear from Ricky's mother, Beth, by email from time to time. She is such a lovely person, and we continue to be grateful for her. Even Ricky's grandparents (on his father's side) each wrote us a lovely letter that will be a wonderful keepsake for Sofie."

In this report, I also spoke of an upcoming home visit on November 17th by Dr. Lyndon Parker from the agency. This visit was an important part of the agency's investigation duties, during which I also received permission to take Sofie out of state to Pittsburgh to visit my mother.

Rachel turned sixteen in November, and she and Ricky came to visit that same weekend. It was an especially fun visit because, at two months old, Sofie was very alert. Finley was clearly the proud sibling, and we celebrated Rachel's birthday with a cake, big HAPPY 16 decorations and lots of laughter and love.

December 17, 1998 — excerpt from third-month report:

"At the time of our last letter, we were looking forward to Rachel and Ricky's visit in November. I am happy to report that the visit was very nice. They both made it, and it was just the two of them. Ricky was so proud to drive to Houston in his new truck. They spent the afternoon, took many pictures and videos, and we had a very pleasant visit. Since then, I have talked to Rachel on the phone a couple of times. Most recently, I called her last week and had the chance to talk with both of them since Ricky was at her house (they are back together and going strong, from what we can tell). She talked about going back to school in January when the new semester begins. She also got permission to try and test out of some courses she missed, and we hope she will be successful in that area. Both of them talked a lot about their jobs at Jack Brown Cleaners. They both work for the same company but at different stores and seem to like the jobs very much. I sent several new photos to them this week. I enjoy sending them pictures because they appreciate it so much. Our next visit is scheduled for mid-January."

In this report, I also mentioned that our nanny, who had been with us since Finley was three months old, would be starting back with us in anticipation of my going back to work. We were grateful that a nanny search was not needed the second time around.

January 23, 1999 — excerpt from the fourth-month report:

"Last Sunday was a scheduled visit for Rachel and Ricky. It turned out to be quite an event. Rachel's mother and father both decided to make the trip to Houston as they were anxious to see Sofia — Kim had not seen Sofia since the hospital. Ricky's parents and siblings also decided to come to Houston for the visit, so there was quite a crowd. Beth thought it would be nice to give us a break from having a houseful, so she invited everyone to meet at her sister's house

in Houston (about a twenty-minute drive from our home). We thought it was a great idea, so plans were initially put in place for all the families to meet at Beth's sister's house. The night before the visit, we got a call from Beth at 10:00 p.m. telling us that Ricky and Rachel had just had a big fight and broken up. They both wanted to see the baby but didn't want to see each other. So, the plans were changed. Rachel and her parents would come to our house in the morning for a visit and then return directly to Austin. Once they left, we were to go to Beth's sister's house to meet with Ricky's family. We thought that would work too. Sunday morning arrived, and we got a call from Kim — they were running late and would not make it in time to see us before we had to leave to go see Ricky's family. So, Rachel decided it would be ok to see Ricky after all. Once everything was straightened out with all parties, the day went just fine. Rachel and her parents did come to our house first, and we spent some nice time alone with Rachel. She got to hold and feed Sofie, and we had a nice, warm visit.

We all then went to see Ricky's family. We arrived late, but everyone was kind and gracious and made all of us feel welcome. Sofia was a real charmer for the "photo shoot" that seemed to last forever. And Finley had a grand time playing with Ricky's eight-year-old sister. Rachel and Ricky did fine too. They spent some time together with Sofie and seemed to be getting along. When it was time to go, emotions were high for everyone. Rachel cried and asked her mom why something so good hurts so bad. We hugged and kissed and went on our way with all the sweet and sad emotions that open adoption brings.

We do not have definitive plans for the next visit; however, we did discuss Rachel and Ricky and perhaps their parents attending Sofia's baptism. It is scheduled for February 14th, and we are waiting to hear from them about this event.

One sad note we have is that Rachel is still not back in school. She went back to her high school for one and a half days but was unhappy. Our understanding is that her parents are trying to find her an alternative school. We just hope and pray that she gets her education."

We also talked about setting the final home visit with Dr. Parker as well as working with the attorney to schedule the adoption court date.

February 27, 1999 — excerpt from the fifth-month report:

"February has been another busy month for our family. Sofia's baptism was on Valentine's Day, and everything turned out perfectly! We had glorious sunshine, and everyone enjoyed the ceremony — even Sofia. She reacted to the first pour of water on her forehead but only with arms up in the air. She never cried, and she smiled for everyone. God was really with us on this day. Rachel and Ricky made it to the church on time and sat right up front with us. Rachel smiled the whole time. It was so nice. After church, our pastor greeted Rachel and Ricky and said some nice things to them. She commended them on making the difficult adoption choice — they both seemed very proud.

After the ceremony, we had everyone over to our house for lunch, lots of photos, and an afternoon visit. This gave us an added benefit of Rachel and Ricky meeting my sister and David's sister and brother. My sister is Sofia's godmother, and she came in from Pittsburgh for the event with her two daughters. David's brother is Sofia's godfather, and he came in from Dallas. It was a day we will remember and cherish forever."

Later, Beth told me how surprised and grateful she was that we invited Rachel and Ricky to Sofie's baptism. It was natural and appropriate for us, especially since we felt so blessed to have Jenna and her sister attend Finley's baptism. But there was a lot more going on than just visiting Sofie. These two teens looked up to David and me, and they wanted to see more of our lives. They even asked us for our opinion on school, life, and career. Beth told me that she was grateful for our relationship because we became role models, and it helped shape her young son in positive ways.

March 16, 1999 — excerpt from the last of six monthly reports:

"Things have been rather quiet with Rachel and Ricky since their visit last month at the Baptism. I did get a note from Rachel this week. She was returning some photo negatives that I had sent to her, and she mentioned that she has been really busy with work and school. She said, "But it is all worth it." We were glad to hear those words. The note was short but nice and upbeat and gave us the feeling that she is still doing well. I also sent her and Ricky some more pictures this week of their visit. I just know Sofia will cherish all of these photos that we have been able to get of her birth family these past many months.

We have also been having a lot of communication with Jenna, Finley's birth mother, these past few months. Jenna is getting married on April 3rd and asked if Finley could be the flower child in her wedding. We gave it a lot of thought and decided that this would be a wonderful gift for Finley. We bought the dress a couple of weeks ago, and Finley can't wait to wear it — tulle and all! We do have a slight concern about them getting down the aisle, but whatever happens will be fine. We also had a concern since Finley has not seen Jenna in over a year, so we asked Jenna if she would plan a visit before the wedding. That is now set for Saturday. It is quite nice of Jenna to make this trip since she now lives in Dallas, but I think she, too, would like to see Finley (and Sofia) before the wedding. With this visit, Finley will feel like they know the bride and will be more at ease. We are really looking forward to seeing Jenna again."

Honestly it was intense. It was a lot to process in the first six months of bringing Sofie home. So much birth family. But I remember that we were happy to see the birth families and especially wanted to connect with the birth parents. Early on, I wanted to get as many memories and pictures as possible because I had no idea what the future would bring and if we would continue to see the birth families in the years to come. The contact made us feel good. We were getting assurance from Rachel and Ricky that they wanted us to parent Sofie, and it was a great gift. When I reflect on the early visits and special occasions with both my children's birth families, I realize those were some of our best moments. For so much of it, we just followed our hearts and our instincts.

In six short months, the time came to make the trip to the San Antonio court to adopt Sofie. I remember the judge was unfriendly. Nevertheless, the adoption went through without a hitch. After he declared us her parents, we asked for a picture, and he complied, but we felt hurried. David and I quickly got up from our seats and went to the judge, holding Sofie for the photo but left Finley sitting with our moms, who had flown in to join us for this glorious day. At that moment, Finley became upset that they were not in the picture, and that has always haunted me for some reason. I hurt Finley's feelings by not scooping them up to get in the picture with us. This is just one of those moments I wish I could get back, redo, and have a family photo with the four of us in that courtroom.

12. Not a Special Aunt

"I felt that you guys adopted me as extended family."

— Jenna, birth mother

After our out-of-state move I learned an important lesson about our family.

In December 1999, about one year after Sofie was born and when Finley was five, we learned that we were being transferred from Houston, Texas, to Fairfax, Virginia, just outside of Washington, D.C. Both David and I worked for the same company, so we were fortunate that our careers could continue with the move. I was so happy about moving because, being from Pittsburgh, the climate and feeling of northern Virginia was as familiar as coming home. It came with a big bonus too — I could actually drive to my mother's house. I wanted my children to be closer to their grandmother. Since David and my mom always got along so well, it was a very happy time for us.

At this point in our birth family relationships, we saw Rachel and Ricky more frequently than we did Jenna. When Finley was a baby, we saw Jenna several times, but by now, Jenna was married and living in a different city, so our interactions were much less frequent. We enjoyed a good healthy relationship with Rachel and Ricky and always looked forward to their baby visits. I recall being concerned about talking to Rachel and Ricky about the move since Sofie was just one year old. I did not want them to think we would abandon our commitment to our open arrangement. Maybe deep down, I thought it might be a little easier for all of us with the distance.

To my great relief, Rachel and Ricky took the news in an outwardly positive way. I say outwardly because, honestly, when I think about it, there is no way they could not have been hurting all over again — they would not be able to just get in a car and come see Sofie. The truth is, it was not just Sofie they came to see. We had grown very fond of one another. They came to know and love our family, and the distance would be a blow no matter what.

But it is my handling of the situation with Jenna that I wish I could do over. I procrastinated in telling her about the pending move, reasoning that we needed to be sure it was a go before we told her. When I finally did, she was gracious, and I was relieved that she had taken the news so well. She was in a different life stage, married, and starting her career in Dallas. I loved Jenna deeply; that was not an issue. We were just in different places in our lives.

I was surprised to get a letter from Jenna about six months after we moved to Virginia, telling us how hurt she was and how she didn't feel part of our family anymore. The way we handled the news upset her. She felt that I had not treated her like family since my mom and sisters had all known about the move well before she did, and that just didn't sit right with her. She said in this letter:

> "One of the things I loved about my decision to go open adoption was the wonderful relationship I developed with you guys. I felt that you guys adopted me as extended family when you adopted Finley. I can't even begin to tell you what that friendship has meant to me in dealing with my grief. I am not very good at calling — but Linda, you always were. Now, I don't remember the last time you called me without my calling you first. Maybe your lives have gotten more complicated with Sofia and your jobs, etc. Had I known sooner about your move, I would've come to visit, and I felt like ya'll didn't even know how much this would alter my life. And how could you know? I don't communicate how I think of Finley 100 times every day. And I haven't been able to go to sleep at night since I found out you were going to move without hurting. Please write back. I love you."

I think that was the hardest letter I have ever read. I, of course, wrote back. Jenna was right; she was and is our family too. I always regretted not giving her the move news much earlier. Someone once said to me that a birth mother might be like a special aunt to my child. I do not think so. She is much more than that and has her own unique role. She is Finley's birth mother and deserved more from us.

13. Making Time

*"I remember as a kid, every time Jenna visited, I would get excited…
I really loved her."*

— Finley, adopted child

Special Visits with Jenna

Thankfully, after the move, Jenna visited us in Virginia. Jenna was always so sweet with Finley, and they loved doing arts and crafts together. She left all the parenting up to us when Finley fussed or wanted extra attention and was respectful of our role as Finley's parents. It was comfortable because Jenna was our family.

I remember having talks with Jenna at some turning points in her life. During one visit, we were walking in the mall — just the two of us. She told me about her job and how she and her husband were doing. They were both working at the same company and putting in a lot of hours. She was doing marketing and communications for her firm and was very proud of her work. I, too, was in marketing and communications at my company, and I thought it was neat that we had that in common. Later, I learned that she went into that field because of me. Jenna then brought up the subject of having children. She said she was not working on it but was also not using birth control. I knew a baby would be coming in the near future!

Jenna is a gifted artist, and during this visit, we were preparing for a birthday party for Sofie as she was turning three. My favorite part of our Virginia home was our large back yard with a great patch of woods featuring fifty-foot-tall pine and ash trees, carpeted with a bed of leaves and long pine needles. We planned to turn the woods in our backyard into the "hundred-acre-woods" and play games at each station. Jenna drew Winnie-the-Pooh characters (Pooh, Rabbit, Tigger, and Ee-yore) on large poster boards. We cut out the three-foot characters, secured them with long sticks to place in the ground and made the game stations. I was always amazed at Jenna's artistic gift and held on to those posters for years because they carried such happy memories.

The next year in 2002, Jenna's daughter was born. A few years later when she was still a toddler, Jenna and her husband came to visit us along with their child. I distinctly remember Jenna's daughter sitting in the highchair at our table and Jenna carefully cutting food for her. I thought she was such a good mother.

Finley and Sofie both enjoyed seeing Jenna and playing with Finley's little birth sister. Interestingly, Sofie remembers this visit more than Finley does. This Memorial Day weekend, we went to our local swimming pool and had fun playing games in the baby pool. Perhaps that visit was more emotional for eight-year-old Finley than I realized. It might have been unsettling for Finley to see their little birth sister, even though it did not seem that way on the surface. This would have been a good time for me to talk more about adoption with Finley. Finley knew that Jenna was their birth mother, and visits were always full of excitement, love, and respect for one another. But I wish we had done more to proactively address any feelings Finley may have had.

Jenna and her husband had moved from Dallas to the Fort Worth area, and they were doing well. Jenna's last visit to Virginia was in the summer of 2006, right before her daughter's fourth and Finley's twelfth birthdays. Jenna wrote me a lovely thank-you letter afterward, telling me how much it meant to her to see all of us again.

They had a second child in 2007. Both Jenna and her husband were working, and his parents lived close to them and helped with childcare. They bought a home and then rented it out and bought a second home to live in. I was thrilled to hear that they were well and stable.

Jenna always sent gifts at Finley's birthday and at Christmas, but understand-ably, traveling to Virginia was hard with two young children, and she could not make the trip again. Her gifts and cards were often handmade, making them all the more special. We continued to acknowledge each other on Mother's Day, too, which was the greatest gift I could ever hope for. They were a busy family, as were we, so it seemed natural that we did not visit each other, especially given the distance between Texas and Virginia. My work required heavy travel at the time, and our weekends were full of sports with both of our children.

Sometime later, I was saddened to learn that Jenna was getting divorced after eleven years of marriage. This was another incredibly hard time for her. She sent me a letter and shared some of the difficult choices she had to make surrounding the divorce and her children.

Finley never developed a relationship with Jenna's two children in the early years. I guess it is not something that Jenna or I worked at making happen. The age difference was so great that it was not a natural fit, and the physical distance was also a barrier. Had we lived in the same city, they probably would know each other well. As I reflect, I wish we had made more time with Jenna and her children as Finley was growing up.

***

Special Visits with Rachel, Ricky, and His Family

Sofie's story included significantly more visits from her birth family during her growing-up years. Looking back, I am grateful for this consistency. While Sofie benefited from these visits, it turns out Finley did too.

Shortly after we moved to Virginia, Beth brought Ricky and Rachel to visit us. They drove from Texas, taking turns driving for twenty-two hours to get to our new home. I have a distinct memory of Beth getting out of the car, obviously exhausted. They stayed just a few days and had to drive all the way back to Texas. Sofie was just one and does not remember this visit, but it was the start of Finley, then five, bonding with Ricky's family. That is when I knew for sure that this family would be part of our family and ours a part of theirs.

I think they must have stayed in a nearby hotel for that first visit. Early on, we were still finding our way with each other, trying not to step on each other's toes, and making visitation as trouble-free as possible. However, after the first visit or two, Ricky's family began to stay in our home when they came. It was easy and felt right.

Ricky graduated high school in 2000, the same year we moved to Virginia, and Rachel graduated the following year. He attended the University of North Wales, Bangor, United Kingdom, to study ecology for a year before returning home to Austin to help support his family. Rachel, who always liked school and was a good student, attended Albright College in Reading, Pennsylvania, on scholarship.

But things were not as settled as they seemed for these two. Rachel and Ricky came to see us in Virginia when Sofie was about two or three. We visited Great Falls National Park for an easy hike along the Mather Gorge overlooking stunning views of the Potomac River falls. Rachel, Ricky, and I took turns holding Sofie's hand to be sure she did not run off, while David tried to keep up with Finley. It was an easy, enjoyable visit, and we were so happy to see both of them, especially Rachel, since she had become a bit more distant.

At the end of our visit, Ricky flew home to Texas, and I recall taking Rachel to the train station in Washington, D.C., so she could head back to college in Pennsylvania. We entered Union Station and were both in awe as we looked up at the soaring ninety-foot arched ceiling adorned with hundreds of octagon coffers decorated in genuine gold leaf. As we moved away from the grandiose main hall and closer to the trains, Rachel's mood change was abrupt. It was as if the drab, industrial feel of the train waiting area matched her unhappy and unsettled frame of mind. It was probably a combination of the end of a visit with Sofie plus the unfamiliarity of going to school out of state that brought her down. Rachel stayed in Pennsylvania for about a year but missed her family in Texas tremendously. I was hoping that since Pennsylvania was relatively close by, we would see her more. But this was not meant to be. She returned to Texas and did not finish college for financial and personal reasons. I can only imagine that not having healed from the trauma of the birth and placement might have contributed to her wanting to go back home.

Beth, Ricky's mom, was the engine that kept Sofie attached to Ricky's family during her growing-up years. She never missed a birthday or a Christmas, and she always sent Sofie a special, personal gift. Each gift included a message from the entire family, such as a picture frame with their names engraved on it, stuffed animals, a soccer ball with their names penned with a Sharpie, or a blanket embroidered with inspirational notes. Every gift was unique and age-appropriate and included everyone — Beth, Mark, Ricky, and each of his siblings. When Ricky and his siblings married, the gifts and messages also included their spouses. They always sent something for Finley too, but Sofie's gifts were very special.

I know this gave Sofie the roots of her birth family, and I always welcomed them with open arms, but I did feel for Finley. While Finley's birth family loved them, they did not get the same attention that Sofie got. I had to balance this and was always concerned about how this attention on Sofie made Finley feel, so I did not fuss too much over the gifts.

We all grew to love Ricky's family. They went out of their way to show love and appreciation toward us. At the same time, they always showed us respect for our role as parents and never crossed that line. Today, even Finley says how much they admire, love, and feel part of this family too.

If you ask him, Ricky will say that he saw his birth daughter at least once a year her entire life. I did not keep track, but this is probably true.

Beth had some roots in Virginia because she had lived there as a young girl. She called one day to say she would be coming to the Washington, D.C. area for a conference and asked if we could meet at her uncle and aunt's home since they lived not too far from us. We were happy to see Beth, so we loaded Finley and Sofie in the car to meet her. I recall the visit being friendly but a little awkward for everyone. That was the only time we saw those relatives. In hindsight, we were all still trying to find the right balance in those early years and went out of our way to respect each other's feelings and territory. I think Beth was just looking to meet somewhere other than our home so that we would not go to too much trouble.

When Rachel and Ricky visited, Sofie always knew these were her birth parents. Visits with them were different than visits from aunts and uncles in that she was the center of attention in a unique way. She also called them by their first names, Rachel and Ricky. I can only recall one time when Sofie asked Ricky for permission to do something, and he naturally, without hesitation, looked at her and said, "You better ask your parents." No confusion there.

Rachel also told me that she remembers visiting Sofie when she was about six. I recall that visit well. We always looked for something fun and unique to do during birth family visits, so this time we went to Virginia's beautiful Shenandoah Valley to tour the Luray Caverns — a magical natural landmark filled with stalactites, stalagmites, and underground reflective pools. Rachel was accompanied by Ricky, Beth, and Ricky's little sister. What Rachel recalls most about the visit was how much fun she had with Sofie and how easy it was to play with her. I have a wonderful picture of Sofie on piggy-back playing with Ricky and Rachel. But as the weekend came to a close, leaving was hard on Rachel. She said Sofie tried to comfort her and told her that she would see her again soon. Rachel was so touched that this little girl felt her pain and tried to make her feel better.

Ricky, too, was doing his own healing and finding his way. After returning from North Wales, he tried a couple of different campuses and finished his undergraduate at UT Austin with degrees in Geography and Ecology. We were invited to his graduation but did not make the trip. Much later, Ricky shared how frustrated he was that we did not bring Sofie to Texas to attend his college graduation. I must admit now that we did not realize how important this was to him. We thought sending a card and gift was the appropriate response. In retrospect, both of us could have done a better job communicating our needs.

During his college years, Ricky proudly posted pictures of Sofie in his dorm room and shared with all of his friends that he had a birth daughter — he proudly shared this fact with any girl that he dated. That was part of his healing process. He even engraved Sofie's name inside his college ring.

Ricky later went on to earn a master's degree in environmental science and went to work for a civil engineering and environmental science consulting firm. That's where he met his fiancée, Lane. All the while, he stayed in touch with us.

Another time, Beth was in Washington, D.C. with her mother, Georgia. We were looking forward to meeting Sofie's birth great-grandmother for the first time, but a major snowstorm came in, making the roads impossible to navigate. There was no way they could make it to the suburbs to see us. However, we did not want to miss the opportunity for Sofie to meet Georgia, and since we had a four-wheel-drive Suburban, we decided we would go to them. The drive was absolutely treacherous, and we should not have attempted it. But the opportunity to meet Beth's mother was too important, so we did. All I can say is that our guardian angels were watching over us because we made it to their hotel and back home safely. It was a drive and visit we will never forget. Later, David told me it was one of the worst winter's drives he had ever made, and that is saying a lot because he grew up in Maine.

When Sofie was about twelve and Finley sixteen, we put together a list of colleges to visit. One of them was UT Austin. Since we were going to Texas, we took the opportunity to visit both Rachel's and Ricky's families separately. By this time, Rachel was married and had two daughters and a baby boy. We met at The Rainforest Café in San Antonio. Rachel came with her three children, along with her sister and her sister's daughter. That day, we also met her older sister for the first time, and both her parents joined us for lunch. It was a big group, and we were thrilled to see them.

Rachel and Sofie sat across the table from one another, and it was a joy to see them interact. Finley stayed close to Sofie and supported her since this was a little overwhelming for young Sofie. Rachel's dad brought Sofie a special beaded elephant since he knew she loved elephants, and she keeps that on her desk today. He also thoughtfully chose a beaded lizard for Finley. Rachel was bouncing her baby boy on her lap most of the time while working hard at concentrating on her conversation with Sofie. It was clear that both enjoyed the visit thoroughly. Sofie loved seeing her siblings and was so sweet with them. She posted a picture from that day of her kneeling down to embrace her two little sisters as they ran to hug and kiss her. She simply loves interacting with little kids. It was loud and noisy and hard to have great conversations, but we were all beaming with pride over our children. Rachel was happy but looked tired and weary, and I worried about her after that visit, though she smiled through it all.

Sometime later, while Sofie was in middle school, Rachel sent us some photos of her children. Sofie proudly posted them on her bedroom mirror so she could see them every day. She remembers texting with Rachel about this time, and one conversation stands out. Sofie had seen a post on Facebook about a young girl being bullied, and she shared with Rachel how upset it made her feel. Rachel responded with some wisdom, "You are just like me; we are both empathetic, bleeding hearts. When I see someone being hurt like that, I feel things as deeply as if it were happening to me." Sofie says that she has always carried that with her, and it makes her feel close to Rachel.

The next year in 2012, we had another opportunity to visit Texas when Finley's birth parents, Jenna and Michael, married (you will read about the wedding in the next chapter), so we took advantage of the time to see Rachel once again. We met for lunch at a restaurant outside of Austin called The Salt Lick. It was a big open, fun Texas barbeque place. This visit was a lot more peaceful since it was just Rachel with her three children, her dad, David, Sofie, Finley, and me. I remember it as a heartwarming, easy visit and Sofie concentrated on coloring and playing with her birth siblings. We were able to talk with Rachel's dad, get to know him better, and understand how much his family depended on him. He thanked us and insisted on picking up the check.

Rachel looked radiant, and Sofie was beginning to look a lot like her. They talked and talked as they both shared the gift of easy conversation. It was a beautiful sunny day, and we took lots of pictures. Sofie had such a good time with her birth siblings, and I remember her little brother hugging her so tight and not wanting us to leave.

One year later in 2013, Ricky and Lane were married, and they invited Sofie, at age fourteen, to be a bridesmaid. It was special for Lane to open up her wedding party to Ricky's birth daughter, whom she had never even met. We were all thrilled, especially because I remembered four-year-old Finley as a flower child in

Jenna's wedding. Lane, a wonderful woman, welcomed Sofie with open arms and made it an enjoyable event for all four of us.

Sofie was invited to the home of Lane's friend to get ready with the rest of the bridesmaids. We dropped her off, thinking all was well since Sofie was always so confident, warm, and friendly. However, it turned out to be a little awkward for her. She was so young and did not know any of the other girls in the wedding party. Of course, they welcomed her, but things were much better for Sofie once she was back with David, Finley, and me.

I was impressed with Ricky's family and their teamwork. I watched as the entire family pulled together and helped with the setup and tear-down of the reception venue at the church. We even joined in to lend a hand. They were all there for each other physically, mentally, and spiritually, and I thought that that was how family should be.

Since Rachel was still in Texas and only about three hours away, after the wedding, we took advantage of the opportunity for Sofie to meet with her birth mom and birth siblings again.

We met for lunch at a local German restaurant and were surprised to learn all about the town of Fredericksburg becoming a wine-producing region in Texas. After lunch and some relaxation, we all went out for ice cream and then enjoyed a walk around the quaint town. Sofie thoroughly enjoyed the time licking ice cream fast enough before it melted with her young siblings and Rachel. It was clear that Rachel was very proud of Sofie.

We met Sofie's birth great-grandmother on Ricky's side, Georgia, for the second time just before Sofie's sixteenth birthday. Georgia's residence had a community room, and Beth arranged for us to meet there for a big catered Texas BBQ meal. Once again, all of Ricky's siblings came. Ricky bought Sofie a pair of beautiful, authentic cowboy boots, just to make sure she knew her Texas roots. It is a gift Sofie still cherishes to this day. She loved sporting those boots around campus and the Boulder, Colorado town.

By this time, we felt part of Ricky's family and had gotten to know and love each of them. And our family, too, had a positive impact on Ricky and his siblings.

It makes me happy to know that we partly influenced his little sister to become an engineer, just like us.

We made another trip to Texas about a year after Ricky and Lane had their first baby. We met at Beth's sister's house — the same place we took Sofie when she was only a few months old. Again, the home was full of relatives and kids with all of Ricky's family. Beth and Mark were especially happy to get a photo with all of their grandchildren — Sofie the oldest at seventeen was holding the youngest, Ricky's one-year-old daughter, in her pretty yellow sundress — while Mark and Beth were laughing as they balanced the other two little grandkids on their laps. Sofie posted this photo on Instagram with the message, "I like how I'm still considered a grandbaby!"

During Sofie's teen years, Beth and Mark had moved to Houston and invited us to their home. It was nice to see them settled in a beautiful home near a running stream. We shared a favorite Mexican fajita meal, and I brought fun, colorful cupcakes from GiGi's Bakery to celebrate. We were familiar and comfortable together, as families should be.

There was a beautiful painting hanging on the wall, and Beth told me that her daughter had painted it. I did not realize that artistic talent ran in the family. I was focused on Finley's artistic abilities, knowing that Finley had inherited them from Jenna. Sofie, too, has artistic flair, and it was not until that day that I realized where it came from.

We took another trip to Dallas in 2016 to visit Ricky and Lane right after their second child was born. He was only a couple of months old, and Sofie was delighted to hold him and play with her little birth sister. And I could see that Sofie developed a special bond with Lane too. Lane once told Sofie that she had only seen Ricky cry twice, and both times were about Sofie. That touched her deeply.

Later that same summer, Sofie graduated high school, and Beth, Mark, Ricky, and his three-year-old daughter traveled to Virginia to attend the ceremony. It was very special for Sofie to have her parents, Finley, her birth father, and birth grandparents at her graduation. This was particularly poignant since both David's mom and my mom had passed away just two years earlier, and Sofie did not have those grandmothers to celebrate with her. They stayed at our home, and we had a grand time. Sofie especially enjoyed painting her little sister's fingernails bright red and sleeping with her baby sister.

When Sofie was a freshman in college, Ricky and Lane planned a ski trip to Colorado and invited her to join them. I helped arrange her transportation to the ski resort as I felt it was important for her to connect with them. Sofie was so excited because she was just learning how to ski. At the end of the trip, they brought her back to campus, where Sofie gave them a dorm and campus tour. It was easy and natural for her to introduce her birth family to her friends.

Then, in 2019, Ricky's sister married, and our family was invited to the wedding. By this time, Finley was still traveling in Asia, but they planned their trip to end in time so they could attend the wedding. This was "family" to Finley, too; they felt welcome and did not want to miss this important event.

***

A Visit with Both Birth Families Together

When I retired, we hosted a dinner in Houston. David and I invited close friends and family, and I was incredibly honored that all three of my sisters flew in for the occasion. Since our children's birth families lived in Texas, naturally, we thought it was a great opportunity to invite them too. I must admit that I was a little nervous but also excited to have both of our children's birth families join, especially since they had not met before.

Jenna and Michael happily attended and sat at our table next to Finley, while Ricky sat at our table next to Sofie. This act of having our children and their birth parents at our table was coming full circle and made David and me so proud. Lane also traveled in from Fort Worth and joined us along with Beth, Mark, and two of Ricky's siblings. Sofie and Finley were both on cloud nine that night, surrounded by so much love from their families.

14. He Matters

Includes special feature by Ricky, birth father

"At that time, I was so disconnected from everything around me. I wanted to be a good person, but I didn't really know what to do or how to do that."

— Michael, birth father

"My greatest hope is that someday when you are older, you will understand this. What we are doing is out of our undying love for you and no other reason."

— Ricky, birth father

When Finley was about six years old, Michael sent us a picture of himself with several buddies from the army. They had visited an orphanage in Korea, and he was thinking a lot about Finley. I showed Finley the picture, though they do not remember it. I didn't take the opportunity to talk about Michael. Maybe I was thinking that Finley was still too young to comprehend it, or maybe it was because they had not expressed curiosity about him. I was not hiding anything; I just thought it prudent to talk more about Michael when Finley was older. Looking back, this was a clear missed opportunity. We never developed a relationship with Michael while Finley was growing up, nor did I talk much about him. If I had to do it over, I would do it differently and proactively bring him up in conversation with my child.

In 2005, when Finley was ten years old, and Michael and Jenna had not yet reunited, Michael married an old high school friend. However, we did not attend the wedding and were never close to them. They had a baby girl in 2007. We exchanged Christmas cards and pictures with Michael and his wife every year, but nothing more.

Sure, there is a huge difference between birth parents; mothers carry the child, attaching to the infant in deep-rooted and profound ways. Because of this, it is natural to be most concerned about the birth mother relationship. But as I have learned through my children's eyes, the birth father is as important as the birth mother, and the children want to know all about him. In hindsight, even a few visits with Michael while Finley was growing up would have helped fill their unspoken need to know more about him.

The same year that Jenna got a divorce, so did Michael.

During Finley's high school years, Jenna and Michael got back together. One Christmas, Jenna and Michael sent Finley a picture of the two of them as a gift. Jenna always had beautiful brown hair, and I remember being shocked at the picture because in it, her hair was a very light blond. Finley did not display the photo in their room; instead, they tucked it away in a drawer. I always wondered why.

In the senior year of high school, Finley wanted to change from brunette to blond hair — the same as Jenna. I'm not sure they connected their hair color choice with Jenna, we never talked about it, but that started a hair color trend for them. Finley has sported every color of the rainbow since then and continues to do so. My favorite during those college years was purple.

In 2012, when Finley was seventeen years old, Jenna and Michael married each other. Jenna told me that she and Michael were soul mates, and I knew this was the happiest time in her life. We were all invited to the wedding and were thrilled to attend as it had been nearly five years since we had seen Jenna and fourteen years since we had seen Michael.

The wedding, held in the countryside near Brenham, Texas, was small and intimate. They said their vows under a beautiful tree, and afterward, we went into a barn for some local homemade food and drink. For decorations, Jenna and her sister sprayed Coke bottles gold and filled them with wildflowers — it was a day filled with love and family.

The most significant thing that happened that day was that Finley met Michael for the very first time. Finley, of course, never remembered meeting him as an infant or at three years old, so this was a big deal. It felt natural to us since we had known Michael from the beginning. However, we did not comprehend the full extent of what it meant for Finley to meet him and his brothers for the first time. Finley did not talk much about it then, but later they did.

We also had the chance to reconnect with Jenna's mom and dad and Michael's dad. And we met Michael's mom and twin brother that day for the first time, too. It was especially fun for Finley to see Michael with his twin and older brother. It was moving, and it felt good and right.

Jenna and Michael spent as much time with Finley as they could during the reception. Their three daughters, much younger than Finley, were at the wedding, too, but Finley was naturally focused on Jenna and Michael. To everyone's surprise, Finley even stood up at the reception and said some words to the group. I can't recall what was said, but I do remember the speech being thoughtful and full of emotion. I thought they were so brave, and I was proud of the young person we had raised. Finley (and me) broke down and cried with a combination of happy and overwhelmed tears. It was a lovely day that passed way too fast.

Somehow, I thought that Jenna and Michael would be more in touch with Finley soon after they married. I think Finley expected that too, but that didn't happen at first. All of us quickly got back to the treadmill of life, Finley was planning a college career, and Jenna and Michael were starting their new life together.

But there were important touchpoints. On one of Finley's birthdays, while they were in college, Jenna sent them a package — homemade coasters made from corkboard with pictures of Jenna and Finley over the years. Finley smiled so big when they showed it to me that I knew how much they cherished this gift.

Since the wedding, Finley has seen Jenna and Michael several times. Once when our family visited David's sister in Houston, we invited Jenna and Michael to visit with us. Jenna and Michael took Finley out to dinner, which was the first opportunity Finley had had to spend any quality time with Michael. Finley came back after dinner delighted and told us that Michael was kind and funny. Michael was honest and shared his struggles with anxiety and depression, and Finley was grateful to get to know him and, in turn, to understand more about themself.

After Finley graduated from college in 2018, they made a special trip to Houston and spent three days with Jenna and Michael. This was the first time Finley slept over at their birth parents' home. I always felt Finley had many unresolved feelings around Jenna and especially Michael and wanted so much for them to spend time together. Michael's twin brother also joined them that weekend. They played games and learned about one another. I know Finley came away from that trip feeling a bond with their birth family. This gave me a lot of peace and happiness. Finley now lives in Austin, and seeing Jenna and Michael is an easy day trip for which we are all grateful.

In November of 2022, Finley was unable to travel home from Texas to Florida to celebrate Thanksgiving with us because they were tied up with work commitments. But something wonderful happened. Jenna and Michael invited them for Thanksgiving dinner and an overnight stay. This would be the first time that they celebrated Thanksgiving together. Twenty-eight-year-old Finley was excited to not only spend time with Jenna and Michael, but also to visit and play with their two-year-old son, Finley's full birth brother.

I was excited for them too because I thought this was a perfect opportunity for Finley to strengthen birth family relationships. When I asked Finley to tell me about the visit, they gushed! Finley is vegan and the whole family went out of the way to have special vegan dishes prepared. Finley's birth grandmother, Susan, prepared a yummy vegan casserole and was especially happy to see Finley. It had been ten years since they had seen each other at Jenna and Michael's wedding.

Later, I also spoke with Jenna, and she said Thanksgiving was a perfect day. She and Michael have three teenage children from previous marriages and two of those daughters were there along with Finley. Jenna was thrilled to see these sibling relationships forming too.

Jenna laughed as she thought about the logistics of serving not only a traditional Thanksgiving turkey meal but also preparing dishes for her vegan and vegetarian children. It was a lot of work, but Jenna would jump at the chance to do it all over again.

***

My interview with Ricky in April 2021 was both the easiest and the hardest of all the birth parent interviews. Since he and his entire family had stayed connected to us since Sofie was born, I wasn't sure how much more there was to learn. In fact, the day I interviewed him was during a weekend visit to our home. Ricky and Lane needed an adult get-away, so they came to stay with us in Florida — just the four of us adults. Sofie was away at college, and Ricky's parents had taken his kids for the weekend, so it was a perfect opportunity to get his perspective.

Ricky reminisced that his and Rachel's teen years were difficult, and their families were very different, which caused a lot of tension. Even though their families did not get along well, Ricky said they did have something in common — they greatly valued family. Rachel and Ricky were kids — just graduating high school was a challenge and a priority.

Ricky shared that he was always getting into trouble as a teen, and he had exhausted his parents. He even recalls finishing some high school classes at a detention center. "We're at school, and we're worried about how we look and our friendships. And so, all of this pregnancy drama is happening, but you know, we're still kids," he said. "The gravity of it didn't sink in immediately; it was kind of like, okay, we are just going to have this baby and do an adoption. As teens, we were very fluid. If anything, we got hung up on the perceptions of what other people thought about us. Rachel being pregnant in school was not easy for her. My friends were pretty supportive, I guess. Some even glorified it as a by-product of living the fast life."

Ricky says much of his teen life is a blur. He thinks his younger brothers and sister probably have fond memories of the neighborhood where they grew up, but Ricky never wants to go back. He wants to leave behind everything that came out of that neighborhood and life in the suburbs. It is one of the reasons he is not attracted to living in the suburbs today — teens with too much time on their hands and not enough inspiration.

He is clear about this — Sofie's birth changed him for the better. "There was a change in me, in my life, and I became very motivated to be something for her," he said. "I told Sofie that I did not sacrifice raising you just to do nothing with my life." It did take time, though. Right after the placement, both he and Rachel were sad, and it took a lot of time to begin healing.

But even after going through all of this with the agency and picking parents for the baby, Ricky said, "We would just get swept back into being kids."

Ricky proactively worked through the healing process over the years by keeping in contact with us, visiting with us when he could, writing about his feelings, and volunteering to help others through BraveLove.org — an organization that shares stories from members of the adoption constellation. I have included the story he wrote for the Brave Love website at the end of this chapter.

I asked Ricky about his memory of finding out Rachel was pregnant. They were together and knew she had missed her cycle, so they got a pregnancy test. He said, "We did the test a couple of times. I remember not believing it, then believing it. Our first thought was that we would have an abortion because we did not want to tell our parents. But then we learned how much that would cost, and we were kids, we had no money, so we had to tell them. We went to a clinic with Rachel's mom and learned about the abortion procedure. That option did not last long."

Ricky remembers standing in his driveway, telling his dad that Rachel was pregnant. He knew his parents were financially stretched, just another issue they had to face, along with their teenage son who was getting into trouble in many ways.

When the idea of adoption was brought up, Ricky recollected that it made sense to everyone. Maybe it was the best thing to do.

"Deciding early to make an adoption plan made the pregnancy a lot easier," said Ricky. "It really relieved some of the stress. The focus became on Rachel taking care of herself, being healthy, and finishing school. That was a lot better than thinking about how on earth we would raise a baby."

Ricky also has some positive memories of the pregnancy. The middle part was a good time in their relationship because they knew what they were going to do. It was kind of freeing. Of course, he was quick to add that the beginning of the pregnancy and the birth were stressful times for them and their families.

He'd had to change his expectations, especially after we moved out of state. It was hard on them when we got transferred from Texas to Virginia. Sofie had just turned one. Ricky said at sixteen, he thought we would be best buds forever, and they would hang out at our house. He had to make peace with the idea that he could not see us often, but he was able to do that because he wanted what was best for Sofie.

In his mind, he rationalized that he could be like a big brother to her if he could not be a dad. As Sofie grew, she became more interested in his perspective and asked for his opinion. He is happy to have that role; it is enough for him.

Ricky commented that his family had to work hard to prioritize the trips to our Virginia home over the years, but even with tight finances, they found a way.

Today, Sofie is an important part of him and his family. So much so that Sofie took a summer internship at his company and spent multiple weekends at their home. I know this didn't happen just by chance. Both of our families worked hard at making this a reality.

When I asked about helping others struggling with decisions about an unplanned pregnancy, Ricky said the best thing you can do is listen. Really listen to people. "I can tell my story, but understand, it is a very personal decision, and everyone has their own unique circumstance," he said. At this time, he offered to speak with other potential birth parents and was able to talk to a struggling birth father, who called Ricky for advice. This was all part of his proactive healing process, and I believe that today, he is more at peace than many birth parents because of this work. He reflected that he and Rachel were so young, and this, coupled with their own family dynamics and beliefs, helped them quickly decide on adoption.

There is no better ending to this chapter on the importance of birth fathers than to read Ricky's own words that he wrote for Brave Love when Sofie was fifteen years old and when he and Lane were expecting their first child:

To the Moon

"It was hard for us and our families, but it was the right choice for Sofie.

Of two things I am certain 1) that my daughter loves me and 2) that I made the right choice. I am a birth father, and fifteen years ago, I chose to place my daughter, Sofie, in open adoption.

When I think back about Sofie's birth and the pregnancy, it's hard to pinpoint any singular moment in time when her birth mother and I decided that adoption was right for us. There was no "lightbulb" moment, no aligning of the stars. It's complicated, and it was hard for us and our families, but it was the right choice for Sofie. I am thirty-two years old now, and it still makes my heart race just to think back about that time in my life.

At only fifteen years old, Sofie's birthmother, Rachel, and I were not unlike other teenage couples faced with an unplanned pregnancy. We were still going to high school, still living with our parents, still trying to discern the meaning of our lives. We were both terrified and knew we weren't capable or ready to provide this child with the stability or guidance that she deserved and needed. Heck, we were still children ourselves! I had just learned how to change the oil in my truck, and my younger sister was still only seven years old.

My parents were still raising their children. Love, however, was never a question. We both loved our precious creation, and we felt the responsibility, the need even, to make sure our child was given every opportunity to succeed, to be loved and protected, and to be cherished above all else.

It isn't that we would not have tried to raise her. We both came from loving families who would have and do cherish her. But we were the birth parents, and we were teenagers, and teenagers make mistakes. They hurt themselves and the people around them. It's just part of growing up. I think even at the age of sixteen, I realized I would continue to fall on my face. Although I could accept hurting myself, I could not accept that my poor decisions might have negative impacts on Sofie's life or that I might neglect her in any way during the trials and tribulations of my teenage years. In my eyes, she was perfect, and she deserved a perfect life.

At some point during the pregnancy, we began to consider open adoption. I knew if I were to forego raising her, I could only be at peace if she knew that I loved her and still wanted to be part of her life. Rachel felt the same way.

As a result, closed adoption was not an option. I did not want her sitting in her bedroom many years later wondering why she had blue eyes, blond hair, braces, flat feet, and a peculiar disposition to saying "y'all" instead of "you guys." I wasn't sure how open adoption would work, but it began to take shape one day at a TGI Friday's in Houston on the faces of two wonderful people that I had never met before. That was the day I met David and Linda, Sofie's adoptive parents. People always talk about those moments in their lives when destiny or fate makes an appearance, and they "just knew it." Well, prior to that visit, I can't recall any experience where I was absolutely sure of anything, but when Rachel and I met David and Linda for the first time, we just "knew it." With the exception of my own parents, there are no two people that I admire more. They have been and continue to be a blessing in my life.

And then came Sofie. She was perfect and amazing, and the world was too full to speak, and so was I. Her little hand grasped my pinky finger, and I smelled her, and I was inspired. That day in the hospital has inspired me for fifteen years — some days more than others, but never far from my heart. Sofie's birth galvanized my life in a way I could have never imagined. I finished high school and college, and I traveled. I lived in different countries, and I learned a new language and how to ride horses. I married a beautiful woman, and today, I installed my very first car seat!

I wanted Sofie to be proud of me. I knew someday she would be sixteen and might wonder why I didn't raise her, and I wanted to be able to say, "See, this is why I couldn't raise you; see how much I had to learn!" and I wanted it to be ok with her.

Thanks to the gracious hearts of David and Linda, I have been able to visit Sofie every year of her life and talk with her a few times a year on Christmas and birthdays. And thanks to my mother, Sofie has always known the love of my family, even during the times when I was lost. Thanks to them, I am not a stranger; I am "Ricky," and Sofie knows my family and my wife, and someday soon, she will meet her sister. I have always been a part of Sofie's life, but I am not her father, and that's ok with me. Sofie is happy, and she is smart, and I know what music she likes and that she's good at field hockey, and I know her dog's name is Cody and that she loves elephants, and I still get to tell her she can't date anyone until she's thirty, and that's enough for me.

Sofie is fifteen years old now, and she is amazing. I know she loves me because she tells me so (in texts with smiley faces). In fact, she loves me "to the moon," and I am so grateful for that. I am expecting the birth of my second daughter, Sofie's half-sister, shortly before this story is to be published. I think about Sofie's birth all the time now, trying to draw parallels between that pregnancy and the one I am experiencing now, trying to conjure up the emotions I felt as a sixteen-year-old kid preparing to be a father. I am still nervous about being a father, but I am ready now.

This story would be incomplete without praising the birth mother, Rachel, for her bravery and sacrifice. I am so grateful to her for her selfless decision; I know how hard it was. Also, thank you to Finley, Lane, Mark, Beth, my siblings, and Rachel's family for loving Sofie as much as I do."

PART V- Growing Up

15. Babies Grieve

"Being adopted has involved losses for children, and they should never be expected to feel grateful ..."

— The Open Adoption Experience, *Melina and Roszia*

When we started on our adoption journey, we thought raising a newborn would be no different than giving birth to that child. They were a clean slate, and we could do the molding, shaping, loving, and bonding. What we did not consider was that the baby had already bonded with their birth mother.

Other than the fact that Finley was the only adoptee among their friend group, the growing-up years were full of many of the same wonderful and fun activities as everyone else's. Elementary school was excellent, and our school benefited from the many parent volunteers that enriched the students with memorable experiences from extra art classes, a renaissance fair, ice skate and pizza bingo nights, to book groups and many more. Life was full of fun camps, piano lessons, scout troop outings, and lots of sports — mostly soccer, basketball, and field hockey. Finley's travel soccer team schedule dominated our household's weekend activities for many years, and we enjoyed deep and lasting friendships with a few other families from Finley's team. Those were exceptionally happy years.

My family and David's family were scattered in different states, but we managed to enjoy great times together with grandparents, aunts, uncles, and seven cousins. For many years my entire family came to our home for Thanksgiving, the year's highlight for everyone — eighteen of us in all. I loved getting the house ready and setting the Thanksgiving table. I would go out to our back yard and collect pine and holly branches with red berries and pinecones to decorate the tables. One year my centerpiece came complete with two spiders making their way across the festive tablecloth resulting in loud shrieks from the kid's table. The cousins especially enjoyed the sleepover in the basement in which they wrote notes back and forth and stayed up half the night.

There were several years that we rented a large beach house in South Carolina to accommodate our families for a week. Sofie, Finley, and all the cousins were close to their grandmother, Grammy, and especially loved that she was always with us for these occasions.

We all have fond memories of our Christmas traditions when David's family came to stay with us too. Having David's mom, Grandy, stay for an extended visit was always a special treat. Even as the children grew older, we still made them wait until Christmas morning to open presents, with one exception. Each Christmas Eve after church and dinner, they opened one gift which was always new pajamas. Never wanting to grow up, especially at Christmas, at ages twenty-two and eighteen, they got matching fleece leopard print onesies complete with hoodies. Finley and Sofie paraded around the living room in their new jammies, singing and dancing.

Our parenting challenges did start early, though. By the time Finley was in the fourth grade, we knew they had some oppositional behavior atypical of children their age. In retrospect, this was near the time of Jenna's visit with her young daughter. It was difficult to know exactly where to turn, so we took them to a counselor. It did not last long, and this counselor did not help. At the time, I never considered that it could have had anything to do with being adopted.

When Finley was ten and Sofie was six, David became a stay-at-home dad. There were many reasons for this but front and center was that Finley was becoming a difficult and oppositional child. We felt it was better to have a full-time parent at home and the stars aligned because David was eligible to take early retirement and my career responsibilities were growing and I was doing a lot of traveling.

Looking back, I realize that Finley was a difficult baby. They were colicky, cried a lot, and were not easy to comfort. We had one of those slider rocking chairs and slider ottomans in the nursery, and we took turns rocking the baby to sleep for hours on end. Inevitably, the moment we set them down in the crib, they started crying. I think Finley came into this world with sadness. I did not understand it at the time, but I believe now that the baby was grieving from losing the comfort and familiarity of Jenna. Finley spent nine months attached to their birth mother in every physical, spiritual, and emotional sense. And according to *The Primal Wound* by Nancy Newton Verrier, while your child has no conscious memory of it, they do have an emotional memory. It can come in unexplained grief or void at any age.

I loved and cared for this precious baby before they were born, in the hospital, and from the moment we brought Finley home. I was sure we had escaped any adoption issues. I was wrong.

Even before they turned one, Finley tried to climb out of the crib. They resisted being confined or put in any "box," which has been a lifetime theme for them. Finley has always resisted norms. To this day, Finley takes pride in a unique quality and style — a trailblazer in every way. Now that I understand much more about non-binary Finley, it is clear that growing up in a world with only boy or girl norms is just too limiting for Finley and so many others. Perhaps some of the oppositional behaviors they exhibited as early as the fourth grade had something to do with being put in a gender box, or perhaps it stemmed from the trauma at birth, or both.

I am grateful that today's world is enlightened about gender identification, and I am working on understanding more about it too. Learning is a process for all of us.

Finley always did well in school and had great friends as the years went by, but they did have difficulties. Finley expressed that they never felt they really belonged to our extended family, that the feeling of being unconnected in some ways was always there. We knew there was a hole in Finley's life, but we did not know what to do about it. We kept them in sports where they excelled, hoping the teen years would go smoothly. But those years were not smooth.

They did, however, stick with sports through most of high school, which provided stability and a wonderful base of family friends. Finley's love of sports became clear early on, especially when they begged us to send them to skateboard summer camp at age thirteen. Later, watching Finley play forward position in soccer and field hockey was a great joy for all of us. Thinking back, I wonder now if Finley's aggressive playing style on the field served to relieve some unidentified frustration. They usually scored a lot!

We got Finley counseling during the high school years, but again, not with an adoption specialist. Finley was diagnosed with ADHD and depression and took some medication. The ADHD medication helped with schoolwork, although Finley was not fond of taking it. They complained that even though it helped them concentrate, it made them feel flat and took the excitement and enjoyment out of life.

The teen years were very trying times for our family, which affected Sofie, too, especially when we had arguments with Finley about friends, curfew, alcohol, and marijuana. We were genuinely concerned for their safety and afraid that they might run away. Fortunately, we had a basement with an extra bedroom and bath, and Finley was able to move to that floor for some much-needed separation. Keeping our child connected to us and safe was our overriding concern, and some separation was the best solution for our family.

Finley's biggest irritant, though, was our security system. Every time a door or window in our home was opened, there was a *ding ding ding*. It was a constant battle, understandably, but it was our way of keeping some control of our teen's comings and goings.

As a high school senior, Finley quit sports, joined a band, and started hanging out with a new group of friends. They always turned to music for happiness, and I think this was a way of seeking a comfortable place. Later in college, they created another band, played the keyboards, sang, and marketed the group. Years of piano lessons in action. When Finley becomes passionate about something, they shine with creativity and skill.

It was not until the year of their twenty-fifth birthday that Finley gently asked us to please use the pronouns *they/them* and explained non-binary identification. This shed light on some of the many feelings and actions growing up. We were not surprised, although we admit that we have a lot to learn about being non-binary. It is also worth noting that Finley told me this is not something you prefer or choose; it is just who you are. Now I understand better. David and I still have work to do on using the correct pronouns easily, but it is becoming second nature with practice. Sofie is a great help in correcting us when needed.

Despite our teen year challenges, there were many positive experiences. Finley surprised us by signing up to take advanced art during their senior year in high school — a first art class since grade school. And Finley excelled. I was stunned at the talent their portfolio revealed. I should not have been so surprised since I knew Jenna was a talented artist. I learned a lesson about making assumptions too quickly.

We sent Finley to an art camp during the summer between kindergarten and first grade. They enjoyed it very much, but I recall inspecting their work, looking for special talent, and thinking their colorful chaotic pieces looked pretty much like all the other six-year-olds. So, we pursued sports for them instead. I could have done more to encourage their artistic talent during the growing up years, but they sure did find it on their own!

Later, David and I often second-guessed ourselves about keeping our children in so many sports. We thought it would be a good way to keep them focused and out of trouble. Did we do the right thing? Should we have explored art for them earlier? David's biggest worry about adoption was not as much a concern about birth parent relationships, but more about confidence in becoming a good father. His own father, mostly absent and not a good role model, never even attended one of his baseball or basketball games while David was growing up. Perhaps this is why he became so involved with his children and coaching their sports. He wanted to do things differently and better than his own father.

Finley graduated from the International Baccalaureate program at their high school, applied to many colleges, and was accepted to most of their choices. They even got accepted into the University of California Los Angeles (UCLA), which was quite a considerable feat. They chose to attend Virginia Commonwealth University Arts. It was the number-one-rated public art university, and it was quite an accomplishment to get accepted into that program. We certainly were proud parents.

Finley realized in college that counseling had been helpful and was still needed. At this point, they lived in Richmond, Virginia, and we lived outside of Washington, D.C. It was, thankfully, only a two-hour drive to see them, and both the accessibility and separation were good for our family. Finley searched and found a counselor that had a lot of adoption experience. This counselor shared the book *The Primal Wound* by Nancy Newton Verrier, which became significant for Finley as it explained abandonment and attachment issues for adoptees. For the first time, Finley could relate to both those feelings. It was Finley that first shared that book with us.

They also tried different medications for depression and ADHD, especially knowing their genetic family history of depression. At a low point during one semester, they needed some more intense help. Their counselor suggested a specific thirty-day in-house program. Finley and I got on a plane to take them to this in-house program, and I packed that embroidered baby blanket that Susan gave to me when Finley was only a month old. Maybe I was finally getting it that adoption might have a role in these troubles.

The program treated a range of issues, and Finley was put in a group with other adoptees. Finley was the only person in that group who had had an open adoption. That was a real eye-opener, and they came out of that program extremely grateful that they knew their birth parents and their story firsthand. When the thirty-day program was complete, they returned to Richmond, focused on their health, finished college, and graduated as part of the honors program. Another proud moment for us.

I see so much of Jenna in Finley. Their smile and laugh are exactly the same, and I hear Jenna in their voice. Also, they both have the most beautiful eyes I have ever seen. I think they both struggle with fitting into the molds this world so cruelly tries to put people into.

Today, Jenna and Michael are both involved with the National Alliance on Mental Illness and spend time advocating for and helping others.

Finley is now an adult, and the relationship with Jenna and Michael is up to them. It is probably not a coincidence that Finley moved back to Texas, where they were born. Finley has an adventuresome spirit and a lot of guts. What is most important to me is that Finley knows love firsthand from both parents and birth parents.

Our relationship with Finley is as strong as ever. Even though we live in different states, not a week goes by that we don't communicate with each other. I am so very proud of Finley and the amazing person they have become.

***

Sofie's growing-up years were similar to Finley's in that she enjoyed all her activities, including Girl Scouts, summer camps, dance, theater, choir, soccer, basketball, and field hockey.

She was also blessed with many good friends. But sometimes those friends were unknowingly hurtful. They would ask Sofie questions like, "Why did your real (birth) parents give you up? Do your real (birth) parents love you?" Because she had experienced first-hand the love from Rachel and Ricky during previous visits, she already knew the answers. She knew why they made the adoption plan. But still, it hurt when friends would ask.

Sofie is bright, and she excelled in school. Her teen years were not without challenges — we had our arguments about friends, alcohol, and marijuana, too. By the time she was in tenth grade, she had begun having some trouble, so we had her evaluated. She, too, was diagnosed with ADHD and anxiety. At first, we were shocked. Since we had been so focused on Finley, we did not expect this from Sofie, who was well-adjusted and seemed to go with the flow of life. Sofie was always a happy, sensitive, and serious student. So, we were not prepared for her teen years.

We were especially stumped by her bursts of anger. Twice she got so angry with us that she punched the wall so hard that she put a hole in it. David, being the reasonable and calm one, took her to Home Depot and had her buy all the supplies — drywall repair patches, spackle, putty knife, and sanding block. He then proceeded to teach her how to patch, sand, and paint a wall.

In talking with Beth, Sofie's birth grandmother, I learned that three of her four children had been on medications for similar ADHD issues. Much later, I learned that anxiety and harboring anger are also challenges common to many adopted children.

We got Sofie the help she needed, and she graduated high school with a full International Baccalaureate diploma. She chose to go to engineering school and was accepted to several programs, including the premier engineering school in Virginia — Virginia Tech, which would have been our choice for her. But that was not where her heart was. Once she learned about the exceptional environmental engineering program at the University of Colorado Boulder, she set her sights on that school. It was not our preference, and in fact, CU Boulder was the only college we chose not to visit with her because we felt it was too far away. Instead, we sent her there, and my sister, who lives in Denver, helped her visit the campus.

Turns out this was her dream school. Sofie came home and put together a PowerPoint presentation, then sat us down to sell us on why this school was the right choice. We could see how much it meant to her, so off she went to Colorado. It also greatly helped to have my sister close by and two cousins going to the same school. This made it much easier for me to let go.

Finley shared much of their discoveries about adoption feelings and issues with Sofie. Sofie continues to benefit from professional counseling in college. We are fortunate that we were able to get both our children this help.

It is amazing to see who Sofie has become. While she is very much her own person, she is an engineer, same as her mom and dad, and an environmental scientist like her birth father. And she has the sweet and gentle disposition of her birth mother.

Sofie and Rachel also keep in touch and talk occasionally. When they get on the phone with each other, I can tell how comfortable they are and I can almost see Sofie's smile when I hear her voice, and I know that Rachel is smiling too. I have often thought about nature versus nurture, and the other day I was looking at an old letter from Rachel. It struck me that her handwriting and Sofie's are almost identical. I find it fascinating that there is a definite genetic component there.

Like with Finley, our relationship with Sofie is as strong as ever now that she is a young adult. The distance between Florida and Colorado is hard on us, but we Facetime each other frequently. Not a week goes by that we don't enjoy our virtual visits immensely.

I found the need to get my children professional help and therapy in the teen years, but I did not relate it to being adopted or any other mental health issues. I was wrong about that. Both of my children acted out and filled voids in some unhealthy ways. Some of it was normal teen behavior, but I believe now that part of it was rooted in the trauma of being separated at birth. Seeking mental help for my children was not easy. I did not talk much to friends and family about it, and I did not interview counselors for adoption experience and expertise. In retrospect, I believe that would have helped. Once the primal wound is acknowledged, the good news is that one can learn how to live and thrive despite the loss, even though it cannot be erased. We learned that our love was not enough to fill that very real void.

I don't recall speaking with my children about adoption. It was just part of who we were as a family and was always presented as a fact — no guilt or shame. We loved connecting with their birth families. Even so, I cannot help thinking that talking more about it, asking the children how they felt about it, and digging a little deeper would have benefitted both them and us as parents. Once my children started therapy, they sometimes said that I should get a therapist too. I was too busy for that, but now I think they were right.

16. Machu Picchu

"No matter how competent and loving the adoptive parents, the child shares no genetic history with them. He is deprived of that primitive relationship…"

— *The Primal Wound*, Nancy Newton Verrier

After Ricky graduated from UT Austin, he spent a year in Mexico, where he had roots on his grandfather's side, learning Spanish and studying wildlife management and sustainable agriculture. I think this may have contributed to Sofie's interest in conservation, and it was the start of her interest in her Hispanic heritage and language too.

Learning about her cultural heritage directly from Ricky was an important way for Sofie to learn more about herself. David's mother was born and raised in Shanghai, China, and came to America when she married David's father in her mid-twenties. Even though our children grew up very close to their Chinese "Grandy," neither child identified themselves with the Asian culture.

Sofie associated herself with her Hispanic roots, especially in her later high school years. Her birth father is half Hispanic, and her birth mother is Caucasian. She has blond hair and blue/gray eyes, so she does not look obviously Hispanic. But any time she filled out a form asking for ethnicity, she wanted to tick the Hispanic box. At first, I thought it was just to ensure her school applications and medical records noted this heritage. But, as I observed, it was much more. Sofie strongly identified with Ricky's trip to Mexico in his early twenties, where he learned about the culture and language, and it has become an important part of her.

After Ricky's return from Mexico, he visited young Sofie in Virginia. This trip also included his father and two brothers. They stayed at our home, and the boys had a great time playing soccer outside with Finley, as Finley was becoming quite the athlete. Sofie was still too young to play soccer with the big boys, but she remembers this visit well. They took Finley and Sofie into Washington, D.C. to visit the monuments, giving David and me a nice afternoon to ourselves. Ricky shared his stories about his time in Mexico, and I am convinced that this influenced Sofie to study Spanish throughout her high school years.

Sofie had dreams of traveling to Spanish-speaking countries as soon as she finished college. She made plans to visit Peru and Costa Rica over the summer before starting full-time work. For her graduation gift, Ricky took her on an amazing trip to visit Machu Picchu in Peru. He wanted that time to bond with her and help her acclimate to the Spanish language before she traveled on her own to other locations to study Spanish and do volunteer work. It was just the two of them for eleven glorious days, with the opportunity to learn things about each other that only this type of adventure can provide.

For me, the real significance is not the adventure, it is the fact that this trip was even possible. It started with a promise twenty-four years ago at the hospital when Sofie's birth mom placed her in my arms. On that day David and I made a promise to Sofie's birth parents that she would always know that it was their immense love for her that led to their adoption decision. We promised that Sofie would always know them.

It was actually Lane who suggested to Ricky that he should take Sofie on a special adventure. They chose Peru not only to see one of the seven wonders of the world, but also because of the Spanish language. Both of them told me that a highlight of the trip was practicing their Spanish together with the tour guides and locals. I love that Sofie was able to have this heritage experience with Ricky, as this is not something that we would have been able to give to her.

Sofie said that this was the first time that she and Ricky were together as two adults and could be unapologetically themselves. They will always remember the thrill of white-water rafting, hiking the magnificent Inca Trail, and they will continue to laugh at how scared they were hanging on for dear life as the bus teetered and bumped along the rough roads and mountain slopes. But the lasting memory will be about connecting with each other. In the evenings before bedtime, without distractions, they were able to share their dreams, their aspirations, and they were comfortable sharing vulnerabilities with each other. This is what they will remember most of all.

As I reflect on this trip, I recognize that the real heroes of this story are Lane and David. Ricky needed to use precious vacation time and Lane, a full-time working mom, would be the one taking care of the kids while Ricky was gone. And David has never wavered about the promise that Ricky would have a relationship with Sofie. I will always be grateful to David and Lane for their selfless acts that made the idea of this incredible trip possible.

17. Big Sister Sofie

"I am so incredibly grateful to my brave parents and birth parents for making the tough decisions they did...because of their courage, I have double the family and double the love! And most importantly, I get to be a big sister to seven perfect humans."

— Sofie, adopted child

I am amazed at the sheer joy on Sofie's face when she visits her young birth siblings. She adores them. Knowing birth siblings while growing up is a gift. There are no preconceived expectations, just a profound connection.

When Sofie was applying for summer internships for 2020, she received three offers. One was from the manufacturing plant where she interned the summer before, one from the company David and I worked for, and one from Ricky's company. For very valid career reasons, she chose the latter. It not only offered what she wanted to learn about as an environmental engineer in water resources, but it also put her in Dallas, close to Ricky and her two siblings. Ricky, Lane, and Sofie had worked hard on Sofie's relationship with the kids, so this was a natural fit. Even though she was an adult at twenty-one, in the middle of a pandemic, it gave David and me great comfort to know she had a safe pandemic pod to visit. Sofie called us to Facetime most weekends, showing us how much fun she was having with her two little siblings. It was a summer full of boat rides on the lake and arts and crafts with the kiddos.

That summer, Sofie was with Ricky on Father's Day for the first time and not with David. She made a heartfelt card for each of them. When Ricky opened his card and read it, he cried. His little girl was puzzled why her daddy was crying, but Sofie knew.

At the end of her internship, I flew to Dallas-Fort Worth so that Sofie and I could drive back to Boulder together before the start of her next semester. I had a relaxed visit with Ricky, Lane, and their kids. By choice, I stayed in a nearby hotel, but Sofie wanted to spend her last night with them. She and Ricky stayed up half the night talking. One of the gifts of our open adoption is that Sofie does not need to worry about hurting our feelings when spending time with her birth parents. When I meet adults who were adopted in a closed arrangement, a common theme is wanting to meet their birth parents, but often there is an overriding concern about not hurting their adoptive parents by searching for birth families. Many decide to wait until their parents are deceased. With open adoption, we did not face any of those complications.

Our relationship with Sofie's birth father continues to be one of love and respect. In early 2021, Ricky, Lane, and their family were headed to Colorado for a ski trip. They invited Sofie to come along, but she was unable due to school commitments. However, Ricky had the idea that maybe they could take a detour on the way and surprise Sofie on a Sunday afternoon. He called David and me and asked if that would be ok. I knew she would love it, but I reflect that he even called us about it. Although Sofie was an adult at twenty-two and they talked freely, he took the time to loop us in and ask our opinion and permission. It was such a sign of respect and love — the way it has always been in our relationship.

There was another visit I recall with Ricky, Lane, their children and our family. When Ricky's five-year-old daughter heard Sofie call David "Dad," she looked confused and said, "but you and I have the same dad." Lane calmly explained to the little one that Ricky is Sofie's birth dad and David is Sofie's dad. That was enough for the five-year-old and no more explanation was needed.

Sofie graduated college in May of 2021. Even though it was a complete virtual graduation event due to the pandemic, David and I traveled there along with Finley to help her celebrate by gathering in our hotel room and watching it on TV. The stars aligned for Ricky and his four-year-old son to be able to fly in for two days and be part of the festivities too. Sofie glowed as she showed off her little brother to her friends.

While Sofie is not as close to her siblings on Rachel's side, they text with each other occasionally. The oldest is now in high school, and her younger sister is in middle school. Sometimes, they ask Sofie for advice. Sofie takes this responsibility seriously. She doesn't want to interfere with Rachel's parenting; she just wants to give the best "big sister" advice possible.

Rachel also has three more children, two of whom we had not met until we made a trip to San Antonio to visit them in July 2021. Seeing how excited Sofie was to see Rachel and all five of her birth siblings, ranging in age from three to fourteen, was simply awesome.

We met at the beautiful San Antonio Botanical Gardens for several hours, which went way too quickly. The day was sweltering hot, but thankfully they had a family adventure section that kept the little ones amused and was the perfect setting for me to get some great candid outdoor photos. Then we enjoyed a meal at a fun Tex-Mex restaurant where Sofie sat in between her two teen siblings and enjoyed the big sis role. Rachel and I talked about raising children and the challenges of motherhood. It was time to go all too soon, and after lots of hugs and a few tears, we were off. Sofie came back and posted some pictures on Instagram with this caption that is so like her:

"I am so incredibly grateful to my brave parents and birth parents for making the tough decisions they did…because of their courage, I have double the family and double the love! And most importantly, I get to be a big sister to seven perfect humans."

Sofie graduated again in May of 2022 with a master's degree. With the pandemic over, she was able to walk the stage this time to accept her degree. Very early on as we planned this event, Ricky told us that he would like to attend her graduation along with Lane and their two children. We were thrilled and knew that Sofie would be delighted to share this day with us and her birth father's family. Before we knew it, Mark and Beth said they were coming too. Sofie is the first of their seven grandchildren, and they were not going to miss it.

Then something remarkable happened, Rachel said she would like to come too. She reflected that she missed a lot of other events as Sofie was growing up and that it would do her heart good to see Sofie graduate from college. We were delighted when she decided to join the celebration too.

Of course, one of the best parts for Sofie was that her big sibling, Finley, came to help celebrate and joined the college crowd at graduation night karaoke and pool bar, while Mom and Dad gratefully went to bed.

As I looked at the group I could not help to think — this is simply the best of what open adoption has to offer. Three families that love my child: our family, her birth father's family, and her birth mother's family. On her graduation day, surrounded by family, friends, and birth families, something struck me. Today is not double the love — it is triple the love.

This same year at Christmastime the stars aligned for Ricky and Lane along with their two little ones to spend a couple of days in Colorado with us. The look of pure joy on the faces of Sofie's little sister and brother when they opened their presents to find t-shirts adorned with pictures of themselves and Sofie along with the words "Big Sis Sofie Loves Me," was priceless.

***

Finley's story with their birth siblings is yet to be written. In June 2021, the pandemic finally seemed to be lifting, so with all of us vaccinated, Finley and I had the confidence to travel to Houston for a visit with Jenna and Michael and to meet Finley's new baby brother for the first time. He would be turning one the next day, and we were both excited and nervous.

It had been four years since I had seen Jenna and Michael and three years for Finley. But the minute we walked in the door, the familiar feelings of love, respect, and excitement to see each other flowed back, as always. When Finley saw their baby brother, they had an immediate visceral reaction, and happy tears flowed. It took me by surprise because Finley is not usually the teary, emotional one in our family (that would be me). It was a tender moment for sure.

As for Jenna and Michael's other children from previous marriages, Finley is looking forward to seeing them again. Although they met at Jenna and Michael's wedding, they did not develop a relationship. Since moving to Austin, Finley has met their siblings a few times. What a gift it may be for them to get to know each other better.

18. Profound Connection

Includes feature interview with my two adopted children

"Talking about adoption with Finley has helped me see our relationship dynamic and understand my sibling better. We are so close now, and it's something I would not change for the world."

— Sofie, adopted child

When Finley was coming up on their second birthday, I told David I thought we should adopt again. He was not so sure. The emotional toll of adopting Finley was significant for him, and, of course, he was now forty-seven years old. He knew it would take at least a couple of years before we were successful. In doing the math — he could be nearly seventy by the time a second child graduated college. But I wanted it so much, and he too wanted a sibling for Finley, so we took a deep breath and started the process all over again. This was one of the best decisions we ever made.

My children have a connection to each other that is more profound than I can truly understand. Their common bond of being adoptees and experiences with their own and each other's birth families has helped them better understand their adoption reality.

For me, the silver lining of the pandemic was having both my children quarantine with us for nearly six weeks. Finley and their partner were headed to Miami for a long weekend vacation. They drove from Virginia and stopped at our home just outside of Jacksonville, Florida. That was March 11, 2020. The plan was to stay with us for two days and continue on to Miami. However, that's when the full force of the pandemic hit, and Miami was the first hotbed area of Florida. So plans changed fast, and they stayed put with us.

A few weeks later, Sofie's university shut down, and she joined us to finish her semester online from home. It was such a mix of fear and joy. Since I had both of them together, I asked if I could interview them for my book. I wanted to interview them individually, but they wanted to do it together. I think this was so they could support each other, as they anticipated that it might bring up some strong emotions.

It took about a month before they were finally ready to sit down for the interviews. I don't know why they hesitated because each of them loved the idea of sharing their stories. Maybe it was just difficult to be interviewed by their mom. The following are excerpts from our discussion.

What is your memory of learning that you were adopted?

Finley: I don't have a specific memory of being told I was adopted. It was just my life. I always knew I was adopted but did not recognize that it was any different from how anyone else lived until, I think, first grade. We had to do a family tree, and I wasn't sure who I was supposed to put on it — you know, that kind of thing.

Sofie: I don't remember when I found out ... I feel like I always knew. I remember you reading me the book *Tell Me Again About the Night I Was Born* by Jamie Lee Curtis. I think that kind of helped me understand adoption.

Do you recall any feelings about being different from friends because you were not living with birth parents?

Finley: It made me feel special and unique. I was always excited to tell people that I was adopted because it made me feel different in a way that was cool. Pretty much my whole life, I always enjoyed being different — feeling unique and special — I enjoyed telling people my story. It was not a conscious source of unhappiness or shame or anything like that.

Sofie: It always bothered me when friends found out I was adopted, and they said, "What about your real parents?" I would always say, "Excuse me, I have two sets of awesome parents — birth parents, and my real parents are the people who raised me." As I grew up, it got a lot more positive. I was able to advocate for myself about what adoption is and get ahead of it instead of letting other people narrate my story for me. So, when I was in a situation where I was supposed to share one fact about myself, it was easy: "I am adopted!" My story got attention, and I would say I have double the family.

What do you remember about visits from your birth families growing up?

Finley: I remember that as a kid, every time Jenna visited, I would get excited — it was so exciting to see her — I really loved her. She always brought a cool present, usually arts or crafts, and we would play. She was a good artist, and we had a lot in common. I remember Jenna's husband at the time would come too, but he was more of a footnote to the experience. I did not bond with him like I did with Jenna.

Sofie: It was so fun and exciting when our birth families would visit. We were the center of attention, and everyone was so excited, and they wanted to hear all about our accomplishments. I remember one time when Jenna and her little daughter came to see Finley and me. We went to the neighborhood swimming pool, and it was really fun playing with Finley's little sibling.

And I remember visits from Ricky and his siblings. It was just fun for me — I always loved being the center of attention. They were so nice, and they brought gifts, and we would play outside in the backyard. They always wanted to play with me and teach me soccer, and it was so positive and enjoyable.

I remember a special visit with Rachel when we met at the Rainforest Café with her three little children. And her mom and dad and sister came too. It was so exciting to see them.

What do you remember about each other's birth family visits?

Finley: As a kid, I felt super jealous. Sofie would get these amazing, personalized gifts. They always brought something for me too, but her presents were so cool! Still, I was super excited to see them, especially when I got a little older and could have a meaningful conversation with Ricky. Getting to know him as a person was important to me. And his family was just so loving and kind; they really welcomed us as part of their family. So, as I got older, the jealousy went away.

Sofie: I was somewhat jealous when Jenna came to visit Finley. I have always been jealous of Finley because they are so impressive. And when you are a little kid, and there are new people around you, you want them to listen to you. But I grew to learn that that was Finley's time with their family and their time to be the center of attention. Our being four years apart helped with that, too. Now, I love hearing about Finley's relationship with Jenna and Michael.

What are your feelings about your birth parents and parents making the adoption choice for you?

Finley: I was never upset with my birth parents or parents for making this choice for me. It's a little like none of us chooses to be born, and the adoption plan was ultimately a good thing.

Sofie: I know that my life would have been different since my birth parents were so young, and that does bring me comfort. I know for me, even right now, there is no way I am mature enough to have a child of my own. So, understanding the situation definitely helps a lot. One of the great things about open adoption was Ricky telling me that not being able to be a dad at that time was a wake-up call, and it allowed him to mature and make some needed changes in his life. He told me about the events leading up to my birth, which put into perspective why the adoption plan was a good decision.

What are your feelings about your birth parents now?

Finley: I feel good about my birth parents now. We don't have a super close relationship, but we are not distant either. We keep up on Facebook. You know, my birth mother is pregnant, and I am going to be a full-blood sibling. So that is a pretty crazy development, and I'm excited to hopefully get to know my new sibling. And the times I have spent with Jenna and Michael in the past have always been great, so yeah, I feel good about them.

Sofie: I'm just grateful that my birth parents are in my life because a lot of people don't have that. It's so nice to see the similarities and differences in the families. I'm going to be working at my birth father's company (although in different offices) this summer, and I am looking forward to seeing more of Ricky, Lane, and the kiddos. At the same time, I am so grateful that I grew up in Northern Virginia with Finley as my sibling. I love my birth family and feel so lucky that they care about me and that they include me. I am big sister Sofie to Ricky's kids, and even though I am a half-sister, they look at me as just a sister. It's interesting to see the similarities in both our birth parents and adoptive parents, and I am grateful that I have them — we have been shaped by both, and what we have is really cool.

What do you remember about telling friends about your birth family?

Finley: All my friends know about my birth family. There was nothing to tell. In our situation, we are so privileged and lucky because not only is our adopted family amazing, but our birth families are amazing, too. There is nothing to hide from other people. There are no secrets. So, it becomes just like a cool, quirky trait of ours, not a huge secret or trauma. So that's all.

Sofie: I talk about it a lot. My friends even teased me about how often I said that I was adopted. I think it's because I am proud of how it's shaped me, and I am happy to share the experience. One of my scholarship advisors was adopted, and we talked about having similar situations. So, yes, I always tell people.

Do you think you are more shaped by nature (genetics) or nurture (how you were raised)?

Finley: I think I am unlike my parents or my birth parents. As a teenager, I felt very different from my adopted family, and learning about my birth family was important to me. It helped me understand that maybe there is a reason I am so different, and it gave me comfort. I just am who I am. I do not think I am more like either family. I do think nurture has more influence than nature does. For me, nurture is the way things happen in your life and how that shapes you. Being adopted is part of nurture and has shaped my identity and perception of who I am.

Sofie: Like my grammy always said, "I am like me." There are some things about my birth family that have shaped me, and there are things about my family that have shaped me. I am a melting pot. I see similarities with my mom and with Rachel — both are caring and sensitive, and anxious, so I can't differentiate who I got that from. And the older I get, the more I learn that there are things about my parents and birth parents that are very different from me, so it is hard to say. I think I learned from Dad things like morals, loyalty, and commitment.

How have your feelings about being adopted changed over time?

Finley: I distinctly remember when I was about twenty-one, I was experiencing a lot of changes in my personality, really growing up and starting to become the person I am. There were things about myself I did not understand, and a lot of them were rooted in the idea of being adopted. A big turning point was reading *The Primal Wound*. I learned that being adopted can affect your attachment to your adoptive family and friends. And that, despite it not being something we can recall, we experienced a feeling of abandonment as an infant and can carry a fear of abandonment that affects our lives. This helped me unlock the puzzle piece of identity missing for me. Essentially, being adopted was this hole or this empty piece, and once I started putting it together, it helped me understand some of my feelings and accept being adopted a lot easier.

One of the family dynamics patterns discussed in *The Primal Wound* is a family with two adopted children. One child tends to be more rebellious (like me, Finley), and one tends to be more of a perfectionist (like my sib, Sofie). And this all stems from the way each child processes a fear of abandonment.

Sofie: Growing up, I couldn't understand what Finley was going through, and I felt on the outskirts. I was uncomfortable hearing about negative feelings, especially in those teen years. Talking about the book with Finley has helped me see our relationship dynamic and understand my sibling better. We are so close now, and it's something I would not change for the world.

What is your current view of open adoption?

Finley: At one point, I went to group therapy, and there were maybe fifteen of us, all adopted. I was the only person in this group who had had an open adoption. To this day, I am the only person besides my sibling that I know of who is in an open adoption. My understanding of open versus traditional adoption is that my birth family was part of my life from the time I was adopted until now.

I think that open adoption is good because it has given me a foundation for understanding who I am in relation to my family and my birth family and accepting being adopted. It changes adoption to being more about love than feeling like someone gave you away or abandoned you. From the eyes of the child, it is a lot easier to grasp that concept of being about love when you feel that love from both your adopted family and birth family. Even as a child, I understood that it was a good decision. I know adoption is about love no matter what, but open adoption makes it easier for a child to understand this.

Sofie: What is so good about open adoption is that I understood it as a young child. I remember being told that my birth parents were really young when they had me, and because I knew the circumstances, I didn't feel like they didn't want me. Sometimes the other kids would ask me why my parents gave me up, and I could explain that my birth parents loved me. When I meet another adoptee who is not in an open adoption, I feel almost guilty that I can have that relationship with my parents and birth parents. I didn't grow up with all those feelings about how my life could be so much different if I were not adopted because I know my story.

What do you see as potential challenges with open adoption?

Finley: I can see where there might be challenges with open adoptions. I think that there are probably many birth parents who make adoption plans because they aren't mentally or physically healthy enough to take care of a child, and I think that could make open adoption really difficult. If a birth parent is struggling with addiction, other mental health disorders, is in a hospital, or in jail, those things might make having a healthy open adoption difficult. It might not even be safe for a child to have a relationship with a birth parent. You might not want to expose your adopted child to those things. All adoptions are challenging, and if you are thinking about adopting, you must accept and face challenges that a lot of other parents don't have. But open adoption is really a great thing for the child.

Sofie: I also think that a challenge to overcome is having a good relationship between the birth parents and adoptive parents. If that trust between the two is not there, things could be difficult. If the trust isn't there, you may not be willing to let the child visit with the birth parents on their own.

What were some of the differences each of you experienced with your birth families?

Finley: I didn't really have a birth father in my life growing up, and that was hard for me. I didn't truly get to know him until I was seventeen, so despite having been openly adopted, I only knew my birth mother. I always felt different from Sofie because she had a relationship with both of her birth parents, and I only had a relationship with one. There was always a part of me that wondered, *Why doesn't he want to see me or do anything with me? Why not send me letters or call me on the phone?* It baffled me. It was always a mystery, like, *Who is this person? Who is my birth father?* Now that I have met him, I know he loves me and wants to have a relationship with me. It was amazing once I met him, but still, all of those thoughts and feelings growing up affected my self-esteem.

Sofie: My birth parents have two totally separate lives. Ricky's wife, Lane, has always accepted me, and Ricky often talked about having a teenage daughter. Ricky's side of the family is big, and I feel part of that big family. My relationship with Ricky is actually stronger than my relationship with Rachel. She always talked to me, and I loved my visits with her, but sometimes I know it was hard for her, and she was so busy with her own kids.

Do you believe divine intervention played a role in your adoption?

Finley: I do not think divine intervention or fate had anything to do with it. I have two great sets of parents who made choices.

Sofie: I have two loving parents who decided to adopt over any other way to have a child and two birth parents who were strong enough to make the decision. I believe that is why we are together, and I am grateful for that. Maybe fate is a better word.

What can you tell me about spending overnights with your birth parents?

Finley: For the first time in twenty-five years, I spent some overnights with my birth parents. It was amazing. We had so much fun. Jenna and Michael are really cool people. We spent the nights playing card games, and we played poker during the day. I got to visit Jenna's office with her. It was a little like the "take your kids to work" days we had growing up. It was cool because Jenna introduced me to her coworkers as her birth child. They already knew who I was, and it was very positive.

One of the things I love is that Jenna and I both tend to need our personal space. When we needed time to ourselves, we didn't need to communicate a lot about it. Everyone got it when we said we were going to our rooms to be alone. We both need alone time to recharge from all the energy spent getting to know each other. It was pretty cool.

Michael's twin brother also visited around that time, but he recently passed away. I am so grateful I had the opportunity to get to know him and spend that time with my birth family. It is so sad that he passed away; it's really hurting the family. But I am grateful that I visited their home at the same time as he did, and the four of us bonded every night.

Sofie: I am so happy that Finley will be able to meet a new birth sibling since Jenna is having a baby soon. One of the things I cherish so much is getting to know my half-siblings when I visit and stay overnight with Ricky and Lane. My little sister and brother are so sweet and special, and seeing how they understand adoption — they don't ask questions. They know I have a different mom and dad and a sibling, and I am just big sister Sofie. I love learning about what Ricky and I have in common, the things he values, and how he deals with being overwhelmed with anxiety and ADHD just like me, and things like that. I appreciate that he shares that with me. And I always love hearing Ricky tell stories about when he was a kid. It is awesome.

What advice do you have for anyone struggling
with a decision about an unplanned pregnancy?

Finley: I do not know what it is like to be pregnant, but I am 150 percent sure that a person should have the choice to do what they want with their body. It is a person's choice, and if that choice is to give birth and they do not feel they have enough resources — mental, physical, material — to raise a child, they could consider open adoption.

Sofie: It's hard because I do not know what it would be like to be in that position. I believe every person has the right to choose and should consider all options of parenting, abortion, or adoption. I would say be honest with your feelings and what you would be comfortable with. If you decide that adoption is right for you, even though it can be wonderful, know that it is not easy. And whether you choose open or closed, your child will wonder about you no matter what, so you might as well just make it easier and have that open relationship. Just be honest and straightforward. Even if you are not ready to be a parent (like being a mom or dad), it does not necessarily mean you are not a parent. You are a person, and they want to know about you, what makes you, you. The adopted child will want to draw those connections.

Do you want to share any final thoughts?

Finley: Read the book *The Primal Wound.* It was introduced to me because I had the privilege of seeing a therapist specializing in adoption. Because she also had an adopted daughter, she knew how to talk to me and get to the root of some of my issues. Don't let your fears stop you from doing what you feel is in your heart. I am very pro-choice. For me, I think having an open adoption has made my heart more loving toward people. I am grateful that I can share my love with my birth mother and adopted mother without it being a competition between the two. Love doesn't run out; there is infinite love to give. Also, having an adopted sister who has her own birth family and having all these families to love has given me an even greater depth to my understanding of people.

Sofie: Make the choice that's in your heart, and don't let anyone push you one way or another. For both birth parents and adoptive parents, I would say just listen, and don't take too much to heart. Be patient about your child's relationship with their birth families. It is not that we love our parents any less or that we are searching for anything else; we're just learning more about our birth families. I think my experience has given me the ability to empathize. You get such a beautiful perspective, and as long as you have a birth family and adoptive family with equal trust, it can be really special. You are giving your child double the love.

***

A Common Bond

My children being exposed to each other's birth families has helped them understand their own adoption stories at a deeper level. The differences in birth family contact as they grew up were significant, but I think each has learned from that. When Ricky's family visited, they always worked hard to pay attention to both children, and they served as role models not only to Sofie but to Finley too. Jenna and Rachel, too, always connected with both Finley and Sofie during their visits, and this helped both children understand how much their parents and birth parents valued the whole family.

Even with all the differences in contact between the four birth parents, both my children ended up in the same place as young adults — with full access to their birth families, deep knowledge of how much their birth parents love them, and multiple good role models in their lives.

PART VI – Birth Family Reflections

19. A Satori Experience

Includes special feature by Jenna, birth mother

*"Open adoption was one of the first things I told people about myself.
It was part of my daily experience."*

— Jenna, birth mother

Throughout the years, I was constantly reminded of how much my children and our family meant to their birth mothers, especially on Mother's Day when Jenna and Rachel reached out to me and I to them. Birth parents can heal, but that does not mean they are moving on from the child. Their birth children and their adoptive families are inextricably linked to them for life.

When Finley and I visited on their little brother's first birthday, Jenna and Michael were as anxious and excited about this reunion as we were. Jenna bought a dozen festive donuts for the occasion, each themed and topped with bright pink, turquoise, chocolate, or white icing and decorated with various kids' cereal or cookie bits and the all-important sprinkles and happy face flags. After singing "Happy Birthday" and indulging, we sat down to chat.

I was especially looking forward to interviewing Jenna and Michael together for this book. Finley sat on the floor, playing with the baby and keeping him occupied while Jenna, Michael, and I reminisced about our time together during Jenna's pregnancy with Finley. Happily, Finley was in the room, taking in the conversation.

I thought I knew Jenna's story, but I learned so much more this day about the depth of trauma she experienced as a teen and how she was able to hide it. I was amazed at how wise and brave this scared sixteen-year-old was.

I found the best perspective of their teen years from a tape Michael had recorded for Finley from his army barracks when he was stationed in Fort Benning, Georgia, in 1997. Finley had just turned three, and Michael planned to come for his first visit to see his child. He wanted us to keep this tape and give it to them as an adult. I had put it away, and I must admit that I forgot about it. I did not know what was on that tape and was thrilled when I found it recently. Of course, finding a twenty-seven-year-old Panasonic tape player so we could listen to it took some doing, but thanks to eBay, we were able to score the equipment. Michael was equally thrilled to know we still had the tape. On it, he told the most tender love story of two teens falling for each other in physical science class their freshman year of high school and later, getting serious in their junior year. He talked about the intense love and excitement they shared when they were together.

Michael described the home Jenna lived in (with her dad and stepmom) as one where she was hardly allowed to leave the house. His home with his mom and brothers was the opposite, with no rules or discipline. He talked about how he first fell in love with Jenna at fourteen and how they wanted to spend every waking moment together. They saw each other in between every class, and he would wait two hours at a Blockbuster video store to spend only forty-five minutes with her before she had to go to work. Then he walked three miles to get home without complaint.

He told the story of how he left his house regularly at 3:00 a.m. many nights to walk three miles to her home just to sneak in and see her, and he never tired of it. He said she was a brilliant poet, an artist, and incredibly beautiful. They were very much in love during the months when Finley was conceived, and they loved Finley deeply. After his breakup with Jenna, Michael described how he longed to see Jenna again. Mostly, he made the tape because he wanted Finley to know that they were conceived out of love.

During our interview, Michael described his feelings as fearful and confused, especially because, at this time, there was a horrific robbery in the home where he and his brother lived with his single mom. Michael and Jenna were in the house, along with his brother and his girlfriend during the event. Drugs and guns were involved, and his brother's girlfriend was accidentally shot in the leg. They were in a bad place and making dangerous choices. Michael was scared to tell his dad about the pregnancy too. When he did, to his surprise, his dad was understanding and advised Michael to support Jenna in whatever decision she made.

Then Michael reminisced about the visit he made to our home when Finley was three and he brought us the tape. At that time, he had already joined the army. Jenna does not remember this visit, but fortunately, I have some pictures. Michael remembers his anxiety was compounded that day because he was going to meet his child. Finley was climbing all over the place — up the back of the couch, just everywhere. "I could not hold them for very long," he said. It was an awkward feeling.

He described himself as immature and uncomfortable. "At that time, I just didn't have any deep, insightful feelings; I was so disconnected from everything around me. I wanted to be a good person, but I didn't really know what to do or how to do that." Looking back, he says that he regrets how he was at that time. "I had to run," he said. "So, I ran."

Michael explained there was a lot he needed to grow into, such as learning who he was and trying to become a responsible person. He looked right at Finley, who was holding their baby brother, and with love in his eyes, said, "No offense to you, but I just couldn't do it. I was so uncomfortable, and I have regrets." At that time, he had a lot of natural anxiety, and he just didn't know how to deal with having a child.

Michael said that he and Jenna never really stopped communicating — mainly through emails, but they sometimes sent mix CDs to each other. Finley was always part of their conversation. He wanted to get his information about Finley through Jenna because he said that he did not have the guts to get it directly from us.

Even though they had broken up and he was in the army, he always yearned to see Jenna again. When he was at Fort Benning, he received a copy of Jenna's wedding invitation. He ripped it up. When he got back from Korea, he tried to contact her, but they didn't see each other again for many years. Eight years later, he was married to his first wife, and they had a daughter.

***

As Jenna talked about this time in her life, she said there were many traumas in her house. It wasn't a place where she felt safe. Her stepmother was mentally abusive, and her dad was gone a lot. She ran away more than once, and her parents always came to find her. But the time finally came when she decided she was not going back.

She said she was stoic and didn't want people to know what she was going through. It wasn't because she was ashamed; it was a defense mechanism, self-preservation. There was this feeling that nobody could know, or she might die. This came from growing up with a dad who was often unkind to her unstable stepmother. If Jenna was too needy or acted out as a squeaky wheel, it could cause rage in the household, leaving Jenna the target of her stepmother's anger. So, she learned to hold it in. After she ran away the last time, her dad and stepmother moved without telling her where they went or how to get in touch. Though she did not want to contact them, she was alone.

When David and I met Jenna and Michael, Jenna was homeless. We did not know this at the time. We knew she was sleeping at the home of a friend and his single mom, but it was not the home we had imagined. She told me that the only meals she had during this time were the free school meals.

Jenna had not lived with her mother, Susan, for years. Susan was hospitalized for mental illness struggles when Jenna was five, and Jenna did not see her again until she was twelve. Jenna now works in the mental health industry and knows how complicated her relationship with her mom was. In many ways, Jenna was the parent to Susan, not the other way around.

Jenna remembers missing her period and getting concerned. They did not have a car, so Michael's older brother dropped them off at Planned Parenthood to be evaluated. When they asked Jenna to go get Michael, she knew right away. Michael came in, and they told them the news together. In shock, Jenna just started to cry. There was so much going on in her world, and she said, "This was the capital event of all the trauma."

Jenna said that she could not comprehend what her future would hold at that time. She was quick to point out, though, that despite all the turmoil, there was also a lot of love. "Michael and I were really in love," she said. "Even though we were scared, I remember him putting his hand on my tummy and saying, 'You know there is a little Jenna and Michael in there.'"

Things started to settle down after the first shock. Michael's mom and brother moved to Alabama after the shooting incident, and Michael moved in with his dad, so he could stay closer to Jenna. But Jenna had no place to go. She moved in with a high school friend of Michael's — someone she did not know well — and felt abortion was her only option. "I didn't have a choice. I didn't know there were other options." Without a home or even a way to feed herself, she could not raise a baby. She said, "Generational trauma stops here." Knowing the trauma in her and her mother's life, she feared for the child she was carrying. She did not want these things to repeat with this child, yet she had no resources to stop that from happening.

Jenna described her experience trying to schedule the abortion. She started calling Planned Parenthood but could not get through. I have to do this now; I want to do this now, she thought. But she began having nightmares and didn't want to do it. Despite calling the clinic multiple times, no one would answer. She was really suffering, so she went so far as to call the Planned Parenthood national hotline in Washington, D.C. She told them the Houston clinic was not picking up. They tried and could not get through either. This was before cell phones, and her access to any phone was limited, so she had to use a friend's landline.

It was shortly after that — either the same night or the next night — that she heard about open adoption. Jenna said, "Yeah, it was cool that I never got through.

It was like a God thing; it was one of those meant-to-be situations." One day, her girlfriend, Parker, was at home watching TV and flipping through channels when she saw some family friends on TV talking about open adoption. Parker's mother contacted the couple on the show. They talked to Jenna, gave her our number, and said to call us. Jenna said she thought it was too good to be true.

Once Jenna and Michael met and matched with us, we provided some financial help through the agency, and Jenna was able to get medical care and move in with her mom. We assumed her mom was helping her during her pregnancy, but Jenna said that while it was better than being homeless, the sixteen-year-old was pretty much still on her own. "You just have to play the cards you are dealt," she said.

That summer, during her pregnancy, Michael moved to Alabama with his mom and brother. It was horrible for Jenna, and even though she was living in her mom's apartment, she felt isolated. The one person that was with Jenna was Finley. "I was so scared of messing up the baby because of my despair."

We then talked about the grief that came after the baby visits. Jenna said, "It is times a gazillion, just really intense." There was a lot about the grief she did not understand. Just when Jenna thought she was doing ok, she would go back for another visit, and those wounds would open up again. "That part was really tough, but it was also healthy," she said.

In her view, the difference between closed and open adoption is that with open adoption, you are exposed again and again to something joyful and painful; you are not shying away from it, avoiding it, or pretending it didn't happen. We talked about how not acknowledging it and keeping it inside means you never heal. I asked Jenna, "Do you think you are healed?" Her answer was, "Well, I am still working on me."

Jenna came to Virginia over Memorial Day weekend when Finley was ten years old. Each year, our town celebrated the holiday by closing off the main street downtown and bringing in carnival rides, games, vendor tents, and food trucks. The whole town attended, reminding me of the movie *Steel Magnolias*. There was not a child that did not look forward to *Viva Vienna!* This was a special year for our family because Jenna would be in town to attend the festival with us. I remember running into friends and neighbors and being a little nervous as I proudly introduced Jenna as Finley's birth mom.

Jenna remembers that visit too, but for different reasons. Finley wanted to go on one of those glider rides where you get strapped in, lying flat on your stomach, and go round and round, flying in your best Superman pose! I suggested she take Finley on that ride, and David and I would take Sofie to a more age-appropriate kiddie ride. Jenna said, "I felt so entrusted. And as I flew around with Finley by my side, it was a satori experience where I was thinking, *Everything is exactly the way it should be.* I just felt uplifted. Like all the baggage I carried was not there anymore. I think in that moment, that part of my life was healed."

I told Jenna that it's hard for me to talk with her about the intense joy we experienced bringing baby Finley into our home. Jenna and Michael had given us this incredible gift of becoming parents, and it was hard to believe we deserved it when she was hurting. Jenna's response again struck a chord in my heart. She said, "You did not have joy because of my grief, and both my grief and my joy coexisted. They all coexisted. One was not at the expense of the other."

When I asked Jenna what advice she had for others with unplanned pregnancies, her response surprised me. She didn't talk about adoption or even the benefits of open adoption. She wanted others to understand the complexities for a teen or young adult in crisis. Specifically, if you are in a crisis pregnancy, then you probably have a lot of other things going on in your world too.

"This person probably needs help and intervention (beyond the pregnancy)," she explained. "There are likely many traumas in her life or around her — things she does not deserve or ask for." Jenna reflects on her situation and can't understand how she was homeless at sixteen, and CPS (Child Protective Services) was not involved. She said, "When my parents moved away, I don't know why no one ever called CPS whenever I got sick at school, and there was no parent to contact. How was that a thing?" As an adult working in the mental health field now, Jenna has reported cases to CPS multiple times. She wants teens to know that help is available to them and that they can find people who care.

Jenna said that open adoption was one of the first things she told people about herself. She said it was rooted and part of her daily experience. In many ways, it helped define who she is today.

I watched Jenna and Finley and saw how comfortable they were together. Finley offered to come for a weekend and babysit their brother, if needed, and all three of their faces lit up at the idea.

Michael reflected on meeting Finley the day he and Jenna married. It was a first-time reunion since he had seen Finley last at the age of three. "I looked at Finley, and it was like wow, there is no doubt in my mind...that is me — that is me right there. And I fell in love immediately," he said.

Jenna laughed, looked at Finley, and chimed in. "Every time y'all talk, like every time he gets off the phone with you, he immediately says, 'I just love Finley. I could talk to them forever.'"

We all laughed and hugged and went out for a lovely dinner. Too soon, it was over, and time for Finley and me to leave. But we were not sad; we were happy because our story is far from finished.

After reading my manuscript, Jenna wanted to write her story in her own words. Her words are so very important. They are a gift to us and to you, dear reader, and I am beyond grateful to Jenna for sharing her very personal, raw, and honest story:

Reading Linda's book is difficult. It's hard for me to even understand why except to say this period of my life was unrelenting suffering. I was swept up in childhood trauma, but I didn't know any better. It was all I had ever known. So, having someone else write about it — having someone else who witnessed it — write about it, is overwhelming.

How do I feel? I feel embarrassed that someone saw me at my lowest. I have feelings that someone is writing MY story...not out of jealousy but because a big part of my story is how goddamn alone I was. I feel so many conflicting emotions it takes my breath away, and I physically cannot read what Linda wrote.

I feel vulnerable and hurt and scared and powerless.

I think what strikes me the most is how Linda didn't know, and still doesn't, how important she was to me. How much I needed a mom to adopt me.

And then, reading this truth I just wrote, I feel surprised and then, of course, immediately judge myself for the need and the feeling.

Right before I found Linda, I remember calling Planned Parenthood. The phone was pale blue and attached to a wall inside my friend Robert's kitchen. It had a long curly cord, and I sat on the stairs and dialed the headset.

Robert's mom was a drinker. And angry. Often angry at me. She said I was an ungrateful whore. But Robert was sweet. He had given up his bedroom and slept on the couch outside the room. He protected me when his mom would get violent. He was letting me stay there due to his friendship with Michael. I didn't have a lot of friends like Michael did. My one friend, Parker, was the only person who had any clue about what I was going through.

My "family of origin" had taught me to keep up appearances at all costs. I was good at it. So, at school, I socialized with a lot of people, was outgoing; I was in advanced classes, my teachers liked me — all the Things.

Of course, my stepmom was verbally abusive, my dad absent. In any case, my home wasn't safe, and I had run away (for the last time) by the time I was fifteen.

And I was in LOVE. Michael was so cool, but in the bad, wrong-side-of-the-tracks sort of way. He had a lot of friends like Robert, who would do anything for him. I would too. I was in love like, fluttery, stammering, wondering if I looked, smelled, and kissed ok.

Michael was living through his own childhood trauma. I held on to him like he and I were the only stable thing in the chaos. As an adult, I'm pretty sure a therapist would call that a trauma bond.

I was sixteen when I found out I was pregnant. I didn't have a full understanding of it because you can't at that age. I knew my life was forever altered in some terrible, scary way. I knew I was not ready.

But I also felt honored. I was in awe of my body and marveled that I could hold life inside me.

Michael seemed to feel the same. We were both scared and knew we couldn't raise a child. But I could see the wonder and love on his face when he put his hand on my belly.

I had a job at Burger King but no car, no health insurance, and no plan. My dad and stepmom had moved months before — I had no way of contacting him even if I had wanted to. My mom had her own mental health issues and was at the time blaming me for the demise of her marriage.

So, there I was, calling Planned Parenthood to schedule an abortion, trying to get it done before Robert's mom got home from work. To be clear, I didn't want an abortion. The idea was wrong, like when you know someone is lying. I couldn't get through — the line just rang and rang.

That night, Parker called me about a new concept she thought might help me. She had been flipping through channels on her TV when she saw someone she knew. A friend of her family was on a talk show discussing how she'd recently adopted a child through open adoption. She explained how the adoptive parents take care of the finances, like prenatal care, and the birth parents can choose to be in contact with the child and adoptive family.

Parker gave me the phone number of the family friend, who, when I called, gave me Linda's number. The first time I spoke with Linda, we talked for what seemed like hours.

I didn't just like Linda. She was who I imagined I wanted to be when I was ready to have kids.

And I loved the concept of openness, that there would not be a moment when my child would be sat down for "a talk" and told they were adopted. I wanted them to know how very loved and special they were to me.

When I told Michael, he said he would support me in anything I chose.

I never even entertained another option after that phone call with Linda. I was relieved not to be having an abortion. Keeping Finley was never an option considering our life circumstances. And even after Linda told me about the adoption process, gave me their "Dear birth mom" letter, and the counselor gave me a book of letters, I never considered any other parents. After I spoke with Linda and met her and David, I knew this was right.

It was shortly after this when Michael moved to Alabama and broke up with me. I don't want to side-track the open adoption story, but, of course, there was more trauma in the chaos. His brother was involved in a shooting when we were at his house, and his mom decided to move the family out of state. At first, Michael moved in with his dad to stay close to me, but a few months later, he moved to be with his brother and mother. Shortly after that, he broke up with me.

I felt utterly abandoned and alone. I lost my only family, my friend, my lover — my moor in the chaos. Life hadn't been easy for Michael or for me, but the open adoption and the circumstances around it were brutal.

On the surface, things seemed bright. Linda and David paid for my expenses, which allowed me to move in with my mom. I stayed in my respectable school. I went to my doctor's appointments.

The truth was, I had no friends. Even Parker distanced herself once I started showing. Teachers, who used to adore me, now treated me like a disgrace. Classmates judged me as a slut. My mom, who had abandoned me when I was six, was gone for weeks at a time. We had no food in the apartment — I ate the free meals at school. I felt physically miserable — swollen, sick, always too hot. I was still a kid, and I was so very alone.

My one joy was Finley. They were my companion. I talked to them, made jokes to them, sang to them.

And I worried that the screaming, the anguish I felt to my core, would hurt them. And it got worse.

Michael came to visit just as I went into labor. It lasted for days. I was emotionally and physically exhausted. But then the baby was born at 11:14 a.m. in November and weighed 7 lbs., 11 oz.

And then it was that I was really, utterly, alone. With a gaping wound, an empty womb. I remember wheeling my IV, lost in the hospital hallways, deliriously searching for Finley, and being led back by a kind nurse.

I held that precious, tiny baby in my arms. I felt like a vessel of God to have produced such a perfect living human.

I watched their new little family — Linda, David, and the baby — from the window of the nursery. I felt warmness in me from that. It was a picture I could hold on to, proof that I did do something right. I did have value.

But the warmth was so fleeting.

That hole, my wound, was not.

I would say that, at least when open adoption is concerned, it is a clean wound. I didn't get the luxury of burying it or avoiding the pain; I reopened the wound and bled it out every time I visited. I got to witness Finley grow up while I, at the same time, was growing up. I grew to love Linda and David more as I became a wife and a mother and as I understood life from different angles.

When Finley was about ten years old, we were at a carnival by their house in Virginia. Finley wanted to go on a ride, but Sofie was too small. Linda suggested I take Finley, and she would take Sofie on a different ride. I was struck then by the specialness of our relationship, by the extraordinary trust we had in one another.

Finley! They were so easy for me to love. What surprised me, what I hadn't expected, was how much I just genuinely liked them. Finley wasn't like other kids I'd met and had to tolerate their look-at-me's and long-winded dream sequences. They were feisty and stubborn and strong and hilarious beyond their years. They had a unique, wry outlook, and they let you know about it.

It was there, in that moment, on the hang-gliding ride, our arms outstretched like Superman, looking over at them, looking over at me, that I felt…whole.

I wasn't, of course. Whole. I mean, I went through a lot of traumas, and it took — is taking — a lifetime to heal. The direction my life has taken led me to have two amazing children, both in their teens now.

I remarried in my thirties. I married Michael, of all people. And let me tell you, he is still a bad boy and still so cool.

When Finley spoke at Michael's and my wedding — I think they were seventeen — there was not a dry eye. You could say things had come full circle.

But then we had a baby, whose first steps at one year old were to Finley. So maybe that's full circle.

What I don't want to gloss over (since I have a socialized tendency to highlight the glossy) is how with open adoption, there were no "winners." Everyone was hurt in this process; not the least of whom is Finley themself. But that's not my story to tell.

I also don't want to give any credence to the "adoption is the option" pro-life groupies. It is an option for some people, and to be clear, no one should be forcing choices on anyone else.

Regarding my open adoption story, I will say this:

1. I am so in love with and proud of who Finley is and is becoming.

2. I am proud of myself for persevering through the difficult path that is open adoption.

3. I am curious to see where the path goes from here.

Warm Regards,

Jenna

20. Changed Lives

"Sofie was the single greatest thing that ever happened to me. It completely changed my worldview, my maturity, everything. Had I not given birth to Sofie, I wouldn't be the person I am today."

— Rachel, birth mother

"There was a change in me, in my life, and I became very motivated to be something for her. I told Sofie, 'I did not sacrifice raising you just to do nothing with my life.'"

— Ricky, birth father

Rachel and I made plans for Sofie and me to come to San Antonio to visit with her family, but we soon realized that we better do the interview for this book by phone ahead of the visit. We both knew that with the excitement of being together again with her family of five children ages three to fourteen, there would be little quiet time to talk. So, we carved out some time in July 2021 for the phone interview.

Rachel started the conversation with concern for Sofie. Since she knew my questions, she had already decided she was going to tell the story about her initial plan to have an abortion. She wanted to know right up front if it would hurt Sofie to know she had even considered this option. I was able to ease her fears because Sofie strongly believes that people should consider all options and choose what is best for their circumstances.

Rachel was also aware that adopted children have a range of feelings about being adopted, and she wondered how Sofie and Finley felt since we had never talked about this before. I told her that both have predominantly positive feelings about being adopted, especially about open adoption, and that I interviewed them, too, so their voices are part of this book. She was happy to hear this.

It is Rachel's nature to be concerned with other people's feelings first. With those fears eased, we began.

In some ways, the hardest part of Rachel being pregnant was what her peers were thinking. She didn't want to be the pregnant girl at school, to get a bad reputation. Even when she tried to go out with a small circle of friends, there was always an influx of new kids, and she always felt judged. She recalls going to a party where a young girl, maybe only thirteen or fourteen years old, started crying and saying, "You cannot give that baby away, that baby needs its mother." Other kids asked her if she was going to have a baby shower. Having random people talk to her and judge her was the hardest. She stopped going to school during the second semester.

After the birth, she and Ricky went to an alternative school. She had a lot of catching up to do, but it was better than going back to the old school. This was a life-changing decision for Rachel because coming back after the pregnancy and adoption plan and dealing with her depression ultimately helped her snap out of some reckless behavior. Her friendship choices at the old school had not been good, and after having Sofie, her mindset shifted. The group they had been hanging with was into drugs and alcohol; they were going down a bad path.

The entire pregnancy experience changed her. She wanted to hold herself to a higher standard, to be someone that Sofie would be proud of. "I didn't know that having Sofia would make me understand love in a whole other way and make me grow up," she said. It was an immediate change. Before this, she had not thought much of potential consequences.

Rachel also reflected that when she met us, she did not want us to know the dysfunction in her life and friend group, for fear we would reject her.

Rachel thinks it's heartbreaking to know that many women, especially teens, facing unplanned pregnancies do not know that open adoption is even a choice. They go straight to abortion as the best solution. And when that happens, it is so much easier just to slip back into what may be an unhealthy lifestyle to ease the pain. For her, carrying a baby for nine months snapped her out of making poor choices, and she is so grateful for that life-changing experience. She wonders where she would be today if she had not gone through with the pregnancy and adoption plan.

Rachel loves her parents deeply, but she feels that some of her teen troubles and pregnancy were due, in part, to her home life at the time. Her parents were unable to pay much attention to her behavior because her mom was dependent on medications, and her dad was busy working, trying to keep the family afloat.

Rachel remembers learning she was pregnant. She and Ricky went into a local grocery store bathroom with a pregnancy test. Once they got over the shock, their immediate reaction was that they needed to have an abortion. When Rachel shared the news with her parents, her mother was particularly concerned about what a pregnancy would do to her fifteen-year-old child and agreed that abortion was her best option.

When they arrived at the clinic, a girl was sitting outside on a picnic bench sobbing. That affected Rachel deeply. She clearly remembers sitting in the waiting room with Ricky and her mom and her name being called. The nurse was very mechanical with her and said that she was the last appointment for the day, and she just wanted to finish her shift. Rachel does not recall any conversation about options.

As they began prepping her, Rachel said, "Stop. I need a moment." Then she got up, dressed, left the clinic, and walked down the street, where her mom and Ricky later picked her up on the side of the road. After comforting her, they were ready to figure out what to do next.

Fortunately, Rachel's mother was familiar with Providence Place because her brother had adopted a child from there. They made plans to contact the agency, and Rachel and Ricky signed up as clients.

Rachel recalled looking through *The Book* of waiting couples and deciding to meet with another family and us. They met with the other family at the mall before our meeting. She told me that it was a perfect contrast seeing both families on the same day.

Rachel and Ricky wanted their child to have a sibling, so they picked two couples with a child. When they met the first couple, their little girl must have been having a bad day because she had a jump rope and kept throwing it at Rachel. Later that day, when they met with us, they were impressed with three-and-a-half-year-old Finley's behavior. Our child had wonderful manners and interacted with Ricky and Rachel so well that they thought, kudos to our parenting! Rachel said it was divine intervention seeing the difference. I smile, too, thinking it really was divine intervention, given how unpredictable small children, including mine, can be. We were fortunate that Finley was having such a good day.

As far as great memories of Sofie's childhood, Rachel said, "There are so many. Every time I came to see you guys, y'all were so gracious. The visits were amazing, and Sofie was always entertaining and sweet. I kept thinking that at some point, she wouldn't want to see me, and you would have to force her. But that never happened. I was beyond grateful for that because nothing was ever forced or manufactured. She was always so genuine."

Every time Rachel visited, she thought that saying good-bye would get easier, but it never did. "The intensity of it all never hit me during the visits, but when it came to saying good-bye, it was really, really hard. It was such a powerful feeling, even though we knew we had another visit scheduled. Sofie was so sweet, and she never wanted to see anybody upset. I remember her comforting me, and saying, 'It's ok, we are going to see each other again soon.' And I was thinking, *You are only six, and you are comforting me!* That's not how it was supposed to be, but she was so great about that."

When thinking about helping other birth mothers, Rachel says, "The first thing I would say is that in today's climate of pro-choice, don't rush to immediately decide to terminate your pregnancy. I'm not saying wait weeks or months, but sit on your decision, and search your heart before you jump into something you might regret for a lifetime. Explore all your choices."

Rachel explained that many people immediately think a teen mom should get an abortion, and they don't even think about the lifetime consequences for the young woman and how she may never heal from that choice. Thinking about adoption, many don't realize that there are options within adoption too. "It may not be right for everyone to be so open, and some may not want to deal with that. But even very young girls need to know about the choices available to them."

Rachel went on to say, "Had Sofie not come into my life, I wouldn't be the person I am today. Even though I placed her because I wanted a better life for her, it also changed me in the process. I honestly don't even want to think where my life would be if not for her." She said, "Having Sofie was the single greatest thing that ever happened to me. It completely changed my worldview, my maturity, everything. It was like night and day."

Rachel learned about open adoption because her uncle had adopted a child. Yet when she went to the abortion clinic, they never even talked to her about other options. They never asked her questions to see if she might be a victim of sex trafficking or if she was being forced to abort. It was just mechanical, and she was treated as nothing more than a number. Rachel wants to be sure there is an open dialogue; it's why she wants this book to be written.

"I could never really have envisioned things going as well as they did with the adoption," she said. She also thinks it is important to be able to talk about how insecure she was at that time, how hard it was to accept the reality, the really hard reality, that "you are not Mommy." It's important to be honest about the loss and learn how to accept it. She knows it is not the right course for everybody, but she could not have envisioned anything better for herself.

She again discussed her irrational fears and insecurities about the open relationship with us, her worry that if she said or did the wrong thing, there would be some switch in our minds, and we would not want her to see Sofie. But that never happened. In fact, it was just the opposite — we wanted to see her more. Thankfully, over the years, her confidence grew.

I asked her about her healing process. Rachel admits that she did not process it or address it as well as she could have. She still harbors some insecurities and wishes that there had been more, better counseling available to her after the placement. It's possible that she has overcompensated for this loss in her life. Her insecurity kept her from sharing more with us. But now, at thirty-eight, she knows she can be herself.

Of one thing she is sure, birth mothers need to have birth mother support groups and grief counseling, and she would advise any birth mother to seek this help.

Rachel is so proud of Sofie. We talked about Sofie's college graduation, her summer internships, and graduate school. Rachel describes Sofie as someone who literally brings sunshine with her everywhere she goes. She is grateful that Sofie has a relationship with her oldest daughters too. They look up to Sofie and think it is the coolest thing to have this big sister.

I tell Rachel that Sofie gets a lot of her kindness and smarts from Rachel, and Rachel says no, she gets all of that from the way we nurtured her. The truth is, it's both.

21. Eighteen Gifts

Includes special feature by Beth, birth grandmother

"We fell into this love story, and my faith in God carried all of us."

— Beth, birth grandmother

The following story was written by Ricky's mother, Beth. Both Beth and I (we are about the same age) went into this arrangement without really knowing how we would navigate our relationship. All we knew from the start was that we felt good about each other and had mutual respect and appreciation for each other's circumstances. It was clear early on that Beth wanted a lifetime connection to her first grandchild, Sofie, but she was also concerned about protecting her son's emotional needs and making sure that he was on a path to healing. Looking back, how we defined "open adoption" together, while not easy, has resulted in much health and happiness for everyone involved. I remain forever grateful to Beth for her wisdom and persistence.

***

Eighteen Gifts for Sofie

I am a birth grandmother. I have started to write my story a million times. I remind myself that I can do hard things. I love our story; it is a faith journey with a happy ending — yet putting the many emotions and memories on paper is challenging. I have always followed my heart, and my nature is to lead with love and optimism. My husband, however, a logical thinker and provider, could imagine no happy ending, so the beginning days were rough. Together we learned that the heartbreaks in life are truly passages to the joys that await you.

"Love is something we abide in, something we fall into — usually when we're out of control, when we're failing and faltering, and we can't do it right. When we reach the end of our resources — and we have to start relying on a power greater than ourselves — that's when we fall into the Great Love that is God."

— Richard Rohr

We fell into this love story, and my faith in God carried all of us.

This is a story of opening our hearts to open adoption, having no idea of the rules, guidelines, or boundaries. Navigating a sixteen-year-old son who was heartbroken, struggling with depression, and yet, a boy we were incredibly proud of for making a decision no child should ever have to make, was difficult. Courageous love is the best way to describe it. We all had to be brave, and I decided from the very beginning this was a family adventure, one we would take together, for better or worse.

After the birth, we were fraught with anticipation of any news of our precious baby Sofie. A picture, a phone call — an email — any news of her! David and Linda were incredibly generous in reaching out, but the loss for us seemed insurmountable. I became a birth grandmother at forty, and I was sad and hurting, something I could have never imagined for my life and something I had no experience with. Thankfully, my son, once he worked through how to handle his grief, took the approach that "if I am going to give up something so precious, then I better make something of my life."

So, the summer of 1999 began a family tradition of making a birthday gift for Sofie. Every year on her birthday, we wanted her to know what a precious gift she was to us and how very much she was loved! There were always conversations and ideas thrown around about what gift, and in some years, more involvement than others, but there was always a gift from her birth father's family. Our goal was a gift we could all sign or participate in making, to give a strong message, "We are here, and we love you."

Looking back, I wish I had done a better job of keeping a journal of this process and photos of the eighteen gifts. It was our way of putting our love in action. It truly is a valuable lesson on how you can nurture relationships and build trust living in different states — or continents, for that matter. When you are the birth family, you tread lightly, not wanting to overstep boundaries and respecting your role. David and Linda were amazing parents, and I think our comfort rested in knowing Sofie knew we loved her. We knew the research was solid on the more positive adults a child has in their life, the greater the chance they would grow up healthy, happy, and successful. We didn't have to have a big part, but we knew we wanted a part.

I can remember the first gift was a baby blanket we all signed. At the time, my youngest child, Georgia, was just eight, and I remember her concentrating so hard to make her signature pretty. We learned that Sofie loved dogs, so one year, we bought her a stuffed dog, and we all signed it. Before long, Sofie was playing soccer, and we signed a soccer ball. As the years went by, signatures always came with notes of love and encouragement.

The three most memorable gifts were a CD of each of our family member's favorite songs on Sofie's sixteenth birthday, a wall sign that read, "You are my favorite hello and my hardest good-bye," and a handmade quilt on her eighteenth birthday with embroidered favorite quotes thoughtfully picked out by each family member. Each of us spent a lot of time coming up with those favorite songs and quotes for Sofie. It was very emotional signing the wall sign because the words rang so true for all of us.

Over the years, each of us visited Sofie in Houston and Virginia, and our relationship was growing and had roots. One especially memorable trip was when Ricky, Rachel, and I drove twenty-two hours to Virginia — just stopping for breaks — to visit Sofie. Looking back, I can remember being exhausted. We were limited on time and funds, but we just found a way.

I greatly valued David and Linda for their love of Sofie, but equally important, their love for our son Ricky. He was young and trying to find his way, and they were important mentors, advisors, role models, and friends in his life. He looked up to them at a time when he was struggling with his relationships at home.

Our gifts to Sofie were our way for her to know us, to reflect our personalities and capacity to love and honor her. They say the manner of giving is more important than the gift. One year, we were all at a waterpark and made paper plates with the words "Happy Birthday, Sofie! We Love You." We each held a plate and then laughed as we took pictures, hot, sunburned, and tired but wishing Sofie was with us.

Truly, family consists of the people who support and love you and the people you trust. Love is given unconditionally, and trust is earned. By the grace of God, our gifts for Sofie in some way allowed her passage into our family and ours into hers.

PART VII – Closing Thoughts

22. Not Yet Earned

"I greatly valued David and Linda for their love…of our son Ricky. He was young and trying to find his way, and they were important mentors, advisors, role models, and friends in his life. He looked up to them at a time when he was struggling with his relationships at home."

— Beth, birth grandmother

"It is important to talk about how insecure I was at the time."

— Rachel, birth mother

Jenna reflected on the impact our relationship had on her. "The reason why our adoption worked was because of the connection you and I had," Jenna said. "I didn't feel like it had anything to do with the adoption agency. In fact, the way I found you guys was not from them. I didn't feel like there was a whole lot of support from them (adoption agency), but I did not have a lot of trust, you know, I didn't trust people."

Jenna had visited us multiple times when Finley was a baby, and I asked her if she ever had any anxiety before seeing us. She said she looked forward to coming any chance she could and anytime she could get a ride. Jenna talked about visiting baby Finley with a broad smile on her face. Then, with tears, she said, "Oh, it was my joy. It was the one thing I was proud of. This was proof that I was a good person. It was the only good thing I'd ever done, you know? And to see this little family, to be part of that, it was just more family than I've ever been a part of. More love than I've ever been a part of. You were an inspiration to me. You were a role model. And the first time we talked on the phone, I thought, *This is who I want to be when I'm ready to have kids.*" (This is the part where I tear up.) Jenna also said the real reason she went into marketing was because I was working in that field. She said I did not know the impact our relationship had on her. There was no one, not even female figures in her life, who had not betrayed her. "So no," she said, "the visits did not cause me anxiety. I loved them."

***

I asked Rachel if she had faith that we would keep our promise for an open adoption, that she would be able to visit Sofie and keep in touch throughout her life. She thought that was an interesting question because she never worried that we wouldn't keep our promise. Her biggest fear was that *she* might push us away, which contributed to severe anxiety before talking to or visiting with us. She described it as an irrational fear that if we saw something in her we thought was negative, we wouldn't want to see her again, or we might think she was a bad influence on Sofie. So that kept her from communicating as much as she wanted to. She was envious of Ricky because he could communicate with us so well. He was always able to be present, to just be himself. She wished she could be more confident in herself.

She thought we went out of our way to keep in contact, and we handled her with grace even when she was very immature and insecure. I told her that at fifteen-years-old, she was amazing. We never saw anything in Rachel that we ever wanted to keep from Sofie.

Today, Rachel sometimes asks me for advice when dealing with her teenage daughters. That will always be part of our special bond.

***

We knew that Jenna, Michael, Rachel and Ricky were seeing us as the ones with a stable, loving home and the wherewithal to provide their child with a good upbringing and education. What I did not fully appreciate at the time was how much they valued us as mentors and role models for their own lives. Now I understand that the responsibility we had to them transcends the relationship with the child. After placement, they had to rely and trust that we would remain open, since our agreement for contact was not legally binding. Looking back now, it is so clear to me that they looked up to us with respect, even when it was not yet earned.

23. Adult Choice

"I always thought at some point I would come to visit, and Sofie would feel forced to see me. That never happened. She was always so genuine."

— Rachel, birth mother

I am a firm believer that life is about the choices we make. Long ago, David and I and our children's birth parents chose open adoption, believing that it was the healthiest choice for the children. We opened the doors to their birth family relationships, but now, it is up to my adult children and their birth families whether they want to continue to walk through those doors and how far they want to go.

As an older parent, I am also comforted by the knowledge that my children and their birth families have the choice to not only remain in contact but also come together without guilt, concern, or the need to hide anything.

The reality is that David and I will likely be gone before my children's birth parents since we are twenty to thirty years older than them. Just as we were given the gift to parent these precious babies so many years ago, we have given the gift of openness back to them. For my children, while I expect that relationships with their birth parents will continue into their adult years, I also hope that some of their birth-sibling relationships will be a joy and comfort to them in the years to come.

Today, Sofie has chosen to have relationships with her birth siblings — both on her birth father's and birth mother's sides. For her, that door was swung wide open by her birth father's entire family all of her life, and it was very natural. She didn't think twice about connecting with her birth siblings on her birth mother's side too. With social media and Facetime, it is easier than ever to stay connected.

For Finley, the door was always open with Jenna but only open a crack with their siblings and Michael during the growing-up years. Today, Finley and their birth family can and do choose to reach out to each other with ease. Since Finley now has a full-birth sibling, they can decide together how to define their relationship. As mentioned previously, I do not think it a coincidence that Finley is back in their birth state of Texas.

The point is there is no correct answer here. It is now all about adult choice, and that's what makes it so special, so right.

24. No Longer Afraid

"You did not have joy because of my grief, and both my grief and my joy coexisted. They all coexisted. One was not at the expense of the other."

— Jenna, birth mother

When David and I decided to adopt a baby and learned that we only qualified if we agreed to an open adoption, we found ourselves in uncomfortable and uncharted territory with little guidance for such a lifelong commitment. We had so many questions. What happens the first year? First five years? Twenty years later? What does visitation between birth and adoptive families look like? Will it be complicated or awkward to raise a child with the birth parents in the picture? How do adopted children feel about this open arrangement?

As you already know from reading our story, we discovered just how much we wanted our children's birth parents and their families in our lives and that it was so crucial for everyone's emotional health — including our own.

When we started our open adoption journey, I knew this would be a healthy solution for the child. Complete transparency about the birth families and the circumstances that led to their adoption made a lot of sense. And while I knew the birth parents would experience the loss of parenting their child, giving them the ability to know and watch their child grow up felt right. I was proud of David and myself for being so willing and accommodating to our children and their birth families. What I did not expect was how much we would benefit, too. We have been immeasurably blessed by the love and respect we share in our birth family relationships. I did not see that coming.

By sharing different genes with our children, it has given us a front row seat to experience natural talents in ways that other families could never imagine. Seeing the artist, outdoorswoman, and chef talents emerge when we are pretty sure they did not get those from either of us, has been a great joy to behold.

Through open adoption, we received the gift of becoming Mom and Dad to two remarkable children. While open adoption did not erase all the issues associated with being adopted and with raising adopted children, it did remove the mystery. Our children never had to wonder if their birth parents loved them or why they made an adoption plan, what their birth parents looked like, or what their family health history or cultural heritage was or even what was the exact day and hour of their birth. Those things were all out in the open, making it easier for the children to deal with their reality.

While we, the birth parents, and the children still needed to work through fears, doubts, sorrow, and loss, open adoption set the stage so that we could develop trusting relationships with each other, and over time we were no longer afraid.

Adoption has changed in the years since we began our journey. Open adoption and semi-open adoption have become the norm. Domestic infant adoption and international adoption have significantly declined in numbers, while the needs of children waiting to be adopted through the foster-care system continue to be great. Not every open adoption will have the benefit we had in matching early and knowing our birth mothers and birth fathers, as well as their extended families. Remaining in contact with each other is something we worked hard at, but we were also fortunate that it was available. Not all adoptions can be that open, especially when they are international or come from complex situations within the foster-care system. Experts today agree that all children can benefit by knowing more about their birth families firsthand. Even if birth parent connection is not possible, adopted children will benefit from any birth family connections with grandparents, aunts, uncles, or other family members. When the child is able to openly celebrate both their nature from their birth family and their nurture from their adopted family it helps them become whole.

My purpose for sharing our story was not only to highlight that open adoption can be a joyful and healthy choice, but also to share the heartache and lessons learned along the way. I hope our story demonstrates that we have been able to lessen the losses that are undeniable and create thriving, healthy relationships. I cannot wait to see how my young adult children and their birth families decide to continue their relationships in the decades to come.

I want to end by conveying my deep respect and love for my husband. David is the most generous and loving father that Finley and Sofie could ever hope for. He has always welcomed our birth families with gratitude, and he holds them dear, but I know it was not always easy. Introspective by nature, he did more listening than talking, and I think that served all of us well.

As a stay-at-home dad, David saw them to the bus each morning, and he was there every day when they came home from school. He coached their basketball and soccer teams for years and never missed a game. He drove their forgotten homework to school on too many occasions and took the brunt of those challenging hormonal teen years. He has always been a rock for them, and when the important life challenges or disappointments came for our children, he was the one who had the calm perspective to get them through.

Open adoption, like most things in life worthwhile, is rarely easy. It takes years to fully understand, and I am still learning. With openness, transparency, and work we have been able to end up in a loving, healing, gratifying and accepting place. Like David always says to Finley and Sofie, "You are where you are and nowhere else, just keep putting one foot in front of the other."

Afterword

While writing and researching for this story, I discovered that some of the biggest shortcomings at the time we adopted was a lack of training for adoptive parents on the unique needs of adopted children as well as structured, proactive support for the birth mothers and fathers after placement. While it is more available now in 2024 than it was thirty years ago, the need remains greater than the resources available to support these groups. **That is why *all* author profits will go towards non-profit organizations that support the unique needs of adoptees and birth parents post-placement.**

According to the American Academy of Pediatrics, all adopted children are assumed to have trauma. A third of adolescents referred for psychotherapy are adopted. Whatever has been gained as a result of adoption does not cancel the real and profound loss of the birth family. Adopted children do experience some level of emotions around abandonment and/or loss and potentially have attachment difficulties. We were fortunate that our open arrangement eased many of the losses, and that we were able to seek professional help for our children.

After placement, even though we settled into comfortable visits and calls with Jenna, Rachel, and Ricky, they were struggling to get on with their lives. We knew that access to our family was an important component of the support they needed, but it was not enough.

Both Jenna and Rachel needed professional help to guide them through the healing process, and neither received it. Jenna is quick to point out that while it was helpful to her to attend the meetings with us and speak about open adoption to the waiting parents group, no one addressed the grief she was going through. We just did not talk about it, and she knows that needs to change.

I also asked Rachel how much support she received after the placement. Similar to Jenna's experience, Rachel felt the support was minimal. Her counselor came to her home a couple of times to see how she was doing, but she does not recall much more. She does remember going into a deep depression after the placement, but she did not reach out to the agency for counseling or support. I gave her Jenna's number, hoping she would connect with her since Jenna had gone through the same thing four years earlier. Rachel called Jenna maybe once but was in such a fragile state that she could not use her as a resource.

The same is true for birth fathers. In the beginning, I naively thought that an unwed expecting father would be relieved when the expecting mother was considering adoption. After all, it removes the burden of child support and potentially messy parenting responsibilities that he certainly did not plan for. But that was before my experience with both of my children's birth fathers, who were thoughtful and involved in making the adoption plan. They too needed professional support post-placement.

Curious to know more about the practice, I met with Providence Place and asked them what support they provide. They said that they are available to birth parents for a lifetime and will help them get the resources needed, *if asked*. It is clear now that Jenna, Rachel, Michael and Ricky would have had to reach out and ask for additional help to receive it. Reaching out for help is not an easy task when you are grieving. And going back to the same place that was central to your trauma, is often not desirable. That is why there is a need for organizations (beyond adoption agencies) that care for people post-placement.

Another changed practice worth noting is the importance of independent representation for expecting parents, no matter their age. In our story Jenna and Michael did not have independent representation when they signed relinquishment papers because the accepted practice was for the same counselor to work with us, the adoptive parents, as well as the expecting parents. Today the best adoption agencies will provide representation and counseling to expecting parents that is separate from adoptive parents.

There are many organizations that support the adoption constellation. Here are three non-profit organizations that provide excellent support:

Boston Post Adoption Resources, Brookline, MA does an outstanding job of supporting members of the adoption constellation and has a focus on making adoptee voices heard.

On Your Feet Foundation, Evanston, IL is a recognized leader in comprehensive post-placement support for birth parents.

Brave Love, Dallas, TX was the organization that helped Ricky tell his birth father story and I believe that helped him heal. They honor and empower birth parents by giving them a platform to share their stories.

Appendix

Dear Birth Parent Letters

Finding Finley

Front:

Dear Birthmother,

We're David & Linda Sexton, and we hope things are going well for you at this time. We admire the courage and strength it must take for you to decide to place your newborn with adoptive parents.

We'd also like to thank you for considering us as adoptive parents. The joy of caring for and playing with our infant nephew and small nieces lets us know, without a doubt, that raising a child, *perhaps your child*, is our heart's desire.

Because of a childhood illness we can't have children of our own, but are grateful that adoption is a wonderful path for us, as well as for you.

The home your newborn would share with us is on a quiet, tree-lined street in a neighborhood called West University Place, in Houston, Texas. And, we'd all attend a small, warm, Episcopalian church not far from here that has some great programs for little ones.

We're both engineers (but not nerds) and although we enjoy our careers in the oil industry our new family comes first. To start with, Linda will take a long leave from work, and David is saving up vacation time, so that we'll be able to establish the important bonds your newborn will need to feel safe, secure, and loved.

During this time, we'll search long and hard for a loving, live-in caregiver to help us when we return to work.

We love our life together, yet dream of what a beautiful addition a child would be. We could go jogging with a jogging stroller. Backpacking in the Rocky Mountains – so much fresh air and sunshine! Linda would have company on the "bunny slopes" when we ski. David would have a new partner for his computer games. And we'd be a real family when we go to DisneyLand!

There would be a child to lick the bowl when Linda bakes. David will have to share! A child to take shopping for school. Linda will have to share! And speaking of school, there's already a savings account for further education, if your child wants.

And we aren't the only ones eagerly awaiting the arrival of an infant. Four sisters and one brother are waiting to become aunts and uncles! Not to mention some very strong and dynamic grandparents, one of them a nurse.

Our pledge as adoptive parents is that your child will know that your strength, your courage and your love allowed him or her to be part of our hearts and our home. We will teach your child to love God, and build his or her self-esteem, so that he or she will always find good and love within, as well as in others.

You must have hundreds of questions about your infant's future with us, and we'd love the opportunity to answer them. So, call us collect, David & Linda Sexton, at (713) 668-4006 or call our adoption advisors at Southwest Maternity Center, 1-800-842-5433.

Sincerely,

David and Linda

David & Linda Sexton

Back

Linda and David celebrate the finish of a six-mile race.

Maybe we'll need a "papoose" carrier the next time we go to Denver.

David & Linda in love ... *forever and ever.*

Linda gets a diploma and big ears.

Our annual Great Pumpkin carving party. Everybody comes. Messy but fun.

David and our niece Lauren. Happy Birthday Lauren!

Finding Sofie

Front

Dear Birth Parent,

Hi! We're David and Linda Sexton, and we admire your courage. We'd like to thank you for considering us as "Mommy" and "Daddy" to your precious baby. Our wish for you is that open adoption brings you comfort and confidence. We know how well open adoption works. Our beautiful daughter Finley, and the special relationship we have with her birthmother is our proof.

We have so much more love to share, that our heart's desire is to grow as a family. We dream of bringing home a new baby to cherish. Not only for us, but so that as they grow, your child and Finley will know the joy of having a brother or sister. Someone to laugh with, play chase with, and to tell fun, silly secrets to.

Linda is very close to her three sisters, all with young families – six cousins for your child! David has a sister and brother who visit often, and your baby will get every bit of their attention.

Family times are big productions (like renting a big beach house), and so much fun, that we want two children to share this with.

Our life is full of fun. Your child will live on a quiet, tree-lined street in West University, Houston, but our home is anything but quiet! We perform puppet shows, make crafts, play in the sandbox and on the slide. And when we're tired of playing at home, we walk to the park down the street.

Our life is filled with very important things too. We will teach your child to love God, and we belong to a small, warm Episcopalian church where Finley has already made many friends. We also think learning should be fun, so our home is filled with toys for the imagination, beautiful music (we love to sing), and wonderful books (a bedtime story every night, sometimes FIVE!). But most important to us, are children to hold, love and keep safe and warm.

Your child will have every advantage we can provide. We both have engineering degrees, and are already saving for his or her higher education.

Our pledge to you is that your child will know that *your* strength, *your* love and *your* concern are the reasons he or she is part of our family. And that there was never a moment when she or he was not loved or wanted.

We know that you care very much about your child's future, so please call, and let's talk with you about your hopes and dreams for your baby. Linda and David at 1-800-530-2455 (access code 66), or call our adoption advisors at Methodist Mission Home, 1-800-842-5433.

Sincerely, *David, Linda and Finley*

David, Linda and Finley Sexton

P.S. Our relationship with Jenna, Finley's birthmother, is built on love and trust. Three years later she still stays in touch with us. She's very excited about our Finley having a brother or sister, and is so content with her choice of open adoption, that she's thoughtfully offered to share her experience with you. She may understand what you're going through better than anyone else. Call us, and we can put you in touch with Jenna, if it will help you in any way.

Back

The Sexton
Family
Photo Album

1. Mom, "Dadoo"
   & Finley.

2. Finley and mom
   are very happy.

3. David & Linda's
   wedding.

4. Home.

5. Finley goes
   blading.

6. Linda & David
   at the lake.

7. Finley makes
   cookies!

Thank you so much
for your time.
Take care and God Bless.

Methodist
Mission Home
1-800-842-5433

Linda & David Sexton
(call collect)
1-713-668-4006

Acknowledgments

When I started writing this book, the best decision I made was to join Amelia Island Writers, a local chapter of the Florida Writers Association. There I found not only help and encouragement, but also friendship. Marla McDaniel and Lee Ann Shobe welcomed me and called me a writer even when I did not feel I earned that title. My dear friend Mollie Bork read and edited every word of my manuscript more times than I can count. My talented writer's group of Rachel Glover, Jane Buyers, and Julia McDermott supported me and helped me to improve along every step of the publication process. Donna Overly and Leslie Kahoun both provided valuable feedback, contacts and endless encouragement. Thanks to all of you for reading my work and keeping me going. You are the definition of Writers Helping Writers.

I am grateful to Alexis Eyler and Kristin Thomas with On Your Feet Foundation and Lori Holden — LavenderLuz.com, for valuable feedback and guidance regarding the complexities of the adoption experience.

Thanks to Providence Place, our adoption agency. Judith Bell, President/CEO and Angelica Cervantes, Chief Program Officer took time on a Sunday morning to meet with Sofie and me in San Antonio, Texas to answer our many questions. Thanks for your patience and support in helping us understand the state of open adoptions today.

I am grateful to my editor, Erin Liles, who helped to shape a more powerful story.

Thanks to the team at Histria for believing in the importance of this story.

This story could not have been told without the love and permission from those who lived it. With deep gratitude I want to thank and acknowledge each of my children's birth parents for agreeing to be interviewed for this book. In doing so, they had to relive a very challenging and difficult time in their lives.

Jenna, you and I began this journey, and we found our way together as path-finders. You said, "Our open adoption worked because of our relationship and for no other reason." Thank you for your love, support and bravery in sharing a story that no sixteen-year-old should need to experience.

Michael, you have been honest and forthright in your description of yourself in those teen years. Thanks for putting it out there so that others can relate. And thanks for your support in helping us to tell our story.

Rachel, when we met you were so young and vulnerable and at the same time incredibly strong and steadfast. Thank you for trusting us and believing in us un-conditionally.

Ricky, you and your family helped define what a healthy open adoption can be. Your deep relationship with Sofie is a testament to what open adoption can achieve. We owe you much love and gratitude.

Beth, you are level-headed, strong, persistent and kind. Your actions through-out the years inspired me to want to write about it. Thank you for showing me what faith in God can do.

Thank you to my sisters Patti, Maureen, and Denise for their constant love and support over the years. Our relationship has taught me the incredible blessings of having siblings to depend on, and inspired me to adopt not once, but twice.

To my sister in-law Barbara and brother in-law David, thank you for being there to welcome our babies home and for your life-long steadfast love and sup-port. And to my brother-in-law Roy for being the creative engine at the very start of this journey.

My children, Finley and Sofie, have been fearless about allowing their stories to be put into words. They never wavered from acknowledging both their struggles and victories so that others can benefit from their story. Thank you for your love, candor, and trust in me.

To my husband, David, thank you for your patience and unconditional sup-port of our life journey and of this book. You are my rock. We did this together.